D1744717

# MENTALLY DISORDERED OFFENDERS

BY

A. E. MUNIR  M.A., Ph.D., Barrister

Dr. A. E. Munir MA, PhD of Gray's Barrister was educated at Brentwood School in Essex and at St. John's College, Cambridge. He was formerly an Under Secretary at the Ministry of Agriculture, Fisheries and Food. He is the author of books on Agriculture and Fisheries as well as European Community Law. He took part in the negotiations for the United Kingdom's entry into the European Communities and the drafting of the European Communities Act 1972 and much of the United Kingdom's implementing legislation of the Common Agricultural Policy.

He now practices as a Barrister at 54 Fleet Street, London EC4, specialising in European Community law, common law and mental health matters.

This book examines the current UK and European legislation on mental health and makes comparisons with the equivalent American legislation. It highlights the problems arising out of the legislation and makes suggestions regarding their solution. It is a useful book for lawyers, psychiatrists as well as social workers and students.

# MENTALLY DISORDERED OFFENDERS

ISBN 1 85863 005 3

First published 1993 by

MINERVA PRESS
2, Old Brompton Road
London SW7 3DQ

Printed in Great Britain
MINERVA PRESS is an imprint of Minerva Press Ltd.

"...that now almost legendary Minerva Press"
George Saintsbury, "The English Novel" (1913) p. 173

# TABLE OF CONTENTS

Table of Cases                                                  viii
Table of Statutes                                               xii

CHAPTER 1: HISTORICAL BACKGROUND                                  1

   1.  Mental Offenders at Common Law                       1
   2.  The Criminal Lunatics Act 1800                       2
   3.  Insane Prisoners Act 1840                            3
   4.  McNaghten's Case                                     3
   5.  Trial of Lunatics Act 1883                           6
   6.  Mentally ill offenders in prison                     7
   7.  Mental Deficiency Act 1913                           7
   8.  Criminal Justice Act 1948                            8
   9.  Mental Health Act 1959                               9

CHAPTER 2: DEFENCE OF INSANITY                                   15

   1.  The defence at common law                           15
   2.  Criminal Lunatics Act 1800                          15
   3.  The McNaghten Case                                  16
   4.  The Butler recommendations                          16
   5.  Comparison of the insanity defence with
       automatism and intoxication defences             19
   6.  The defence of automatism                           19
   7.  The test of recklessness                            21
   8.  Defences as mitigating factors                      24
   9.  Unfitness to plead                                  24

CHAPTER 3: DEFENCE OF DIMINISHED RESPONSIBILITY 26

   1.  Introduction of defence                             26
   2.  Judge or jury                                       27
   3.  Defence to prove diminished responsibility          28
   4.  Problem with timing of defence                      29
   5.  Success of defence                                  30
   6.  Continuing need for the defence                     30

| | | |
|---|---|---|
| 7. | Circumstances when defence available | 31 |
| 8. | Reduction in hospital orders | 32 |
| 9. | Proposal for reviewable prison sentences | 32 |
| 10. | Conclusion | 32 |

CHAPTER 4:  AMERICAN COMPARISON     34

| | | |
|---|---|---|
| 1. | Brief background | 34 |
| 2. | Model penal code | 35 |
| 3. | Constitutional constraints | 36 |
| 4. | Diminished capacity | 36 |
| 5. | Diminished responsibility | 39 |
| 6. | Burden of proof | 40 |
| 7. | Sentencing of insane offenders | 41 |
| 8. | The Durham formula | 42 |
| 9. | The Hinckley case | 42 |
| 10. | Possible developments in light of American cases | 44 |

CHAPTER 5:  ANALYSIS OF THE 1982 AMENDMENTS     48

| | | |
|---|---|---|
| 1. | New definitions | 48 |
| 2. | More frequent access to tribunals | 49 |
| 3. | Extension of powers of Mental Health Review Tribunals | 50 |
| 4. | Transfer directions | 51 |
| 5. | Consent to treatment | 52 |
| 6. | Consent to treatment under the Mental Health Act | 55 |
| 7. | Treatment requiring consent and second opinion | 55 |
| 8. | Treatment requiring consent or second opinion | 56 |

CHAPTER 6:  HOSPITAL ORDERS UNDER 1983 ACT     58

| | | |
|---|---|---|
| 1. | Requirements for hospital orders | 58 |
| 2. | Medical recommendations | 60 |
| 3. | Suggested improvements to the hospital order provisions | 63 |
| 4. | Hospital order cases | 65 |
| 5. | Decline in number of hospital orders | 70 |
| 6. | Improvements to medical recommendation requirements | 72 |
| 7. | Possible breach of statutory duty | 73 |

CHAPTER 7:  RESTRICTION ORDERS UNDER MENTAL
            HEALTH ACT 1983                                      76

    1.  Requirements of restriction orders                       76
    2.  Problems with restriction orders                         77
    3.  Possible amendments of requirements for
          restriction orders                                     82
    4.  Restriction order cases                                  83
    5.  Cases tried at the Old Bailey during 1984                83
    6.  Proposed reforms                                         87

CHAPTER 8:  MENTAL HEALTH REVIEW TRIBUNALS                       91

    1.  Establishment of Tribunals                               91
    2.  Changes included in the Mental Health Act
          1983                                                   91
    3.  Appointment of members of tribunals                      92
    4.  Applications to tribunal                                 93
    5.  Automatic reviews                                        94
    6.  References to a tribunal by the Home Secretary           94
    7.  Proceedings before the tribunal                          95
    8.  Tribunal decisions                                       98
    9.  Powers of tribunals                                      99
   10.  Problems with Mental Health Review Tribunals            101
   11.  Suggested improvements                                  102

CHAPTER 9:  CONCLUSION                                          104

    1.  Reform of the defence of insanity                       104
    2.  The meaning of mental illness                           107
    3.  Proposed definition of ''severe mental illness''        108
    4.  Diminished responsibility                                110
    5.  Hospital orders                                          110
    6.  The role of psychiatrists                                110
    7.  Law Commission proposals                                 112

NOTES                                                           113
INDEX                                                           131

# TABLE OF CASES

Attorney General v. Associated Newspapers [1989] 1 WLR 322 101
Associated Provincial Picture Houses Ltd v. Wednesbury
    Corporation [1948] 1 KB 223    74
Benham v. Edwards (1982) 678 F2d 511    120
Bone v. Mental Health Review Tribunal [1985] 3 All ER 330    99
Bourne v. Norwich Crematorium Ltd [1967] 1 WLR 691    130
Browner v. United States (1972) 417 F2d 969    42
Curry v. State (1981) 611 SW 2d 745    42
Davis v. United States (1985) 160 US 469    40
Durham v. United States (1954) 214 F2d 862    42
Furman v. Georgia (1972) 409 US 238    120
Grant v. Mental Health Review Tribunal
    The Times April 26 1986    99
Gregg v. Georgia (1976) 428 US 153    39
Hendershott v. People (1982) 653 2d 385    38
Hinckley Case (1981) 525 F Supp 1342    42-44, 45, 46, 47
Home Secretary v. Mental Health Review Tribunal
    for Mersey R H Authority [1986] 3 All ER 233    100
Jackson v. Indiana (1972) 406 US 715    41
Jones v. United States (1983) 103 US 3943    44
Korsak v. State (1941) 154 SW 2d 348    35-36
Kynaston v. Secretary of State for the Home Department
    (1981) 3 Cr App R 281    80
Leland v. Oregon (1952) 343 US 790    40
Lyles v. United States (1957) 254 F2d 725    41
McNaghten Case (1843) 10 Cl & Fin 200    3-6, 10, 16, 18, 23,
    24, 25, 31, 34, 35, 42, 44, 45, 46, 47, 67, 104, 106, 110, 112
Meade v. Haringey LBC [1979] 1 WLR 637    74
Pickering v. Liverpool Daily Express and Echo Newspapers
    The Times January 18, 1990    101
Parsons v. State (1987) 81 Ala 577    35
People v. Drew (1978) 22 Cal 3d 333, 149    35
People v. Henderson 60 Cal 2d 750    37
People v. Poddar 10 Cal 2d 750    37
People v. Skinner 18 US (para 20)    47
People v. Thompson (1979) 591 P 2d 1031    41

People v. Wolff (1964) 61 Cal 2d 795                                      37
Powell v. Texas (1968) 392 US 514                                        36
R v. Arnold (1724) 16 St Tr 695                                           2
R v. Arrowsmith [1976] Crim LR 636                                       87
R v. Bailey [1983] 2 All ER 503                              19, 20, 21
R v. Bennett [1968] 2 All ER 753                              .   77, 87
R v. Blair  Unreported                                                   85
R v. Bluck (1730) Old Bailey Sessions Papers 10                           2
R v. Bow (1733) Old Bailey Sessions Papers 33                             2
R v. Buck (1730) Old Bailey Sessions Papers 13                            1
R v. Burgess [1991] 2 All ER 769                                         17
R v. Burles [1970] 1 All ER 642                                          25
R v. Byrne (1960) 44 Cr App R 246                             16, 31, 111
R v. Campbell (1987) 84 Cr App R 255                                     28
R v. Cox (1968) 52 Cr App R 130                                      27, 67
R v. Judith Defour (1733) Old Bailey Sessions Papers 82           115
R v. Ahmed Din (1962) 46 Cr App R 269                                    28
R v. Dix (1982) 74 Cr App R 306                                         115
R v. Dixon (1868) 11 Cox CC 341                                           6
R v. Duca (1959) 43 Cr App R 167                                        117
R v. Egdell  The Times December 14, 1988                                102
R v. Evans  The Times October 20, 1984                                   68
R v. Fish (1985) 7 Cr App R (S) 310                                      88
R v. Fisher (1981) 3 Cr App R (S) 112                                    88
R v. Ford (1976)  Unreported                                             27
R v. Frances (1849) 4 Cox CC 57                                           5
R v. Gardiner [1967] 1 All ER 895                        78, 79, 83, 85, 87
R v. Greenberg [1974] Crim LR 236                                        72
R v. Gunnel (1966) 50 Cr App R 242                                   71, 86
R v. Hadfield (1800) 27 St Tr 1281                                    2, 15
R v. Hallstrom ex p W (No. 2) [1986] 2 All ER 306                        53
R v. Hardie [1984] 3 All ER 848                                          22
R v. Harding  The Times June 15 1983                                     64
R v. Harvey and Ryan [1971] Crim Lr 664                                  72
R v. Harvey [1988] Crim LR 241                                           30
R v. Hatt [1962] Crim LR 647                                         59, 129
R v. Higginbotham [1961] 3 All ER 616                                71, 80
R v. Hurse (1984)  Unreported                                            83

ix

R v. Richard Johnson and Benjamin Keys (1729) Old Bailey
   Sessions Papers 11      1
R v. Iandolo (1984) Unreported      84
R v. Kay The Times May 11, 1986      81, 101
R v. Kemp [1957] 1 QB 399      24
R v. Keys (1730) Old Bailey Sessions Papers 16      1
R v. Kooken (1982) 74 Cr App R 30      29
R v. Leyton (1849) 4 Cox CC 149      6
R v. Lincoln (Kesteven) Justices ex p O'Connor [1983]
   1 WLR 335      59
R v. Matheson (1958) 42 Cr App R 145      27
R v. McFarlane (1975) 60 Cr App R 320      67
R v. Magnolia The Times January 14, 1988      73
R v. Mental Health Act Commission ex p W The Times
   May 27 1988      57
R v. Mental Health Review Tribunal ex p Clatworthy [1985]
   3 All ER 699      99
R v. Mental Health Review Tribunal ex p Home Department
   The Times March 25, 1987      101
R v. Mental Health Review Tribunal ex p Pickering [1986]
   1 All ER 99      101
R v. Mizon and Darker (1984) Unreported      86
R v. Morris (1961) 45 Cr App R 379      32, 65, 66, 67
R v. Oxford Regional Mental Health Tribunal [1986]
   3 All ER 239      93
R v. Porter The Times January 22, 1985      68, 69, 70
R v. Quick [1973] QB 910      20, 23
R v. Ramsgate Justices ex p Kazmarek (1984) 80 Cr App R 366   59
R v. Robertson [1968] 3 All ER 557      25
R v. Simpson (1984) Unreported      85
R v. Sullivan [1984] AC 156      6, 17, 19, 22, 23, 24, 25, 104
R v. Sturgeon (1738) Old Bailey Sessions Papers 108      2
R v. Tandy [1988] Crim LR 308      118
R v. Tinto (1984) Unreported      62, 73
R v. Toland (1977) 58 Cr App R 453      85
R v. Turner [1975] QB 834      110
R v. Turner (1984) Unreported      85
R v. Vinagre (1979) 69 Cr App R 104      27

R v. Wells (1984)  Unreported                                    84
R v. Yorkshire Mental Health Review Tribunal [1986]
    3 All ER 239                                             95, 128
Re Walker's Application  The Times November 26, 1987             74
Re Winship (1970)  397 US 358                                    40
Secretary of State for the Home Department v. Oxford
    Mental Health Review Tribunal [1987]  3 All ER 8    81, 95, 128
State v. Nuckolls (1980)  273 SE 2d 87                           41
State v. Strasberg  60 Wash 106                                  36
T v. T and Another  The Times May 25, 1989                      54
Taylor v. State (1982)  440 NE 2d 1109                          40
Taylor v. United States (1954)  214 F 2d 398                    41
Unwin v. Hanson [1891]  2 QB 119                               130
Walton v. R (1977)  66 Cr App R 25                             28
W (a minor) v. Dolbey [1983]  Crim LR 681                      22
W v. L [1973]  3 All ER 884                                89, 107
Winterwerp (1979)  2 EHRR 387                                50, 89
Woolmington v. DPP [1835]  AC 462                              15
X v. United Kingdom (1981)  4 EHRR 18144, 48, 50, 51, 80, 81, 91

# TABLE OF STATUTES

1800 Criminal Lunatics Act (39 & 40 Geo 3 c94)          2, 3, 15, 41
1840 Insane Prisoners Act (3 & 4 Vict c54)                       3
1861 Offences Against the Person Act (24 & 25 Vict c100)        20
1879 Summary Jurisdiction Act (42 & 43 Vict c49)                 7
1883 Trial of Lunatics Act (46 & 47 Vict c38)                    6
1890 Lunacy Act  (53 & 54 Vict c5)                        8, 9, 61
1907 Probation of Offenders Act (7 Edw 7 c17)                 7, 8
1907 Criminal Appeal Act (7 Edw 7 c23)                           6
1913 Mental Deficiency Act (3 & 4 Geo 5 c28)            7, 8, 9, 70
1927 Mental Deficiency Act (17 & 18 Geo 5 c33)                8, 9
1930 Mental Treatment Act (20 & 21 Geo 5 c23)                    9
1946 National Health Service Act (9 & 10 Geo 6 c81)              9
1948 Criminal Justice Act (11 & 12 Geo 6 c58)                 8, 9
1957 Homicide Act (5 & 6 Eliz 2 c11)         9, 10, 16, 17, 26, 29,
                                                        31, 37, 110
1959 Mental Health Act (7 & 8 Eliz 2 c72)      9-14, 18, 48, 51, 59,
      60, 65, 66, 67, 70, 71, 80, 82, 83, 90, 91, 98, 104, 107, 109
1964 Criminal Procedure (Insanity) Act (c84)         6, 17, 24, 31,
                                                        45, 93, 94
1971 Criminal Damage Act (c48)                          21, 22, 85
1973 National Health Service Reorganisation Act (c32)           11
1973 Powers of Criminal Courts Act (c62)         9, 18, 68, 69, 70
1977 National Health Service Act (c49)                          73
1981 Contempt of Court Act (c49)                               101
1982 Mental Health (Amendment) Act (c51)      14, 48-57, 81, 104
1983 Mental Health Act (c20) 3, 10, 12, 14, 16, 18, 26, 32, 36, 44,
   45, 47, 51, 53, 54, 55, 58, 61, 64, 68, 69, 76, 77, 78, 79, 80, 82,
83, 84, 87, 89, 90, 91, 92, 93, 94, 98, 99, 100, 101, 102, 103, 105,
                                          107, 108, 109, 110, 112
1985 Housing Act (c68)                                          63
1991 Criminal Procedure (Insanity and Unfitness to Plead) Act (c25)
                        17, 24, 31, 45, 47, 104, 105, 110, 112

# MENTALLY DISORDERED OFFENDERS

CHAPTER 1:  HISTORICAL BACKGROUND


## 1. Mental offenders at Common law

It was accepted from earliest times at common law that insane offenders could not be executed.[1]  Hale, writing in the 17th century, assumes that originally the defence of insanity was thus limited to capital offences.[2]    No evidence can be found to question this assumption.  It was not until the middle of the 18th century that the defence came to be accepted for non-capital offences.[3]  It has been suggested[4] that this may be attributable to the growing importance of transportation at that time as a substitute for hanging.  While it is true that at the beginning of the 18th century by far the commonest punishment at the Old Bailey was transportation, there is also evidence that by the 1720s the defence of insanity was accepted for all types of crime.  As it was accepted without question at the time, it could well be that it was fully established prior to the 1720s.

In the Old Bailey Sessions Papers of 1729 for the First Sessions in the mayoralty of Sir Richard Brocas 89 prisoners were indicted, of which 8 were sentenced to death; 2 to be whipped and 33 to transportation.  Thus by far the largest group was sentenced to transportation.  There was only one case in those Sessions involving insanity: *R. v. Richard Johnson and Benjamin Keys.*[5]  Keys had confessed that he and Johnson had robbed Samuel Tyson.  Evidence was presented that Keys was a "crazy fellow" and "when in drink he would talk of things false and groundless and charge himself with crimes he never did."  Keys was acquitted on that ground.

In the Third Sessions in 1730, 85 prisoners were indicted of which 10 were sentenced to death; 6 to be burnt in the hand; 3 to be whipped and 32 for transportation.

There were two cases involving insanity.  One was Robert Keys[6] again, who this time confessed to shooting John Newton and was acquitted.  The other case was *R. v. William Buck*[7] who was indicted for stealing a chest and carpenters' tools; but it appearing by several evidence that he was a crazy distracted person he was acquitted on that ground.

Throughout the rest of the century, the most common sentence at the Old Bailey was that of transportation.  Pleas of insanity, which were sometimes accepted and sometimes not, were not limited to only capital offences.  On occasion, a plea of insanity was accepted on what would these days be regarded as quite flimsy evidence, such as the behaviour of the offender in the dock[8] or what impression the keeper at his gaol formed as to his mental condition.[9]

While the Old Bailey Sessions Papers are by no means anything like conclusive evidence of what happened throughout the country for all offences in the 18th century, nevertheless they are some guide, and perhaps the only systematic guide, which is available of the trends in the treatment of mentally disordered offenders at the time. Official Statistics did not become available until about a century later.

*R. v. Arnold*[10] established that the question to be put to the jury was whether the prisoner "knew what he was doing and was able to distinguish whether he was doing good or evil and understood what he did." Arnold was found guilty as he was not "totally deprived of his understanding and memory." Although there was evidence that he suffered from delusions. In *R. v. Hadfield*[11] the prisoner was acquitted of attempting to assassinate George III "he being under the influence of insanity at the time the act was committed." The court accepted his Counsel's submission that there did not have to be a total deprivation of understanding and reason before the defence was available. It was sufficient that the prisoner suffered from delusions. Thus by 1800 the defence was extended to delusions.

## 2. The Criminal Lunatics Act 1800

The Act of 1800 related to those who were charged with high treason, murder or felony but were found to be of unsound mind at the time of committing the offence and thus acquitted although it was dangerous to permit them to go at large.

Section 1 provided that in those circumstances the jury should be required to find specially whether such person was insane and to declare whether he was acquitted by them on account of such insanity. If they so found then the court was required to "order such person to be kept in strict custody, in such place and in such manner as the court shall deem fit, until his Majesty's pleasure be known." It would then be lawful for his Majesty, obviously acting on advice, to give such order for the safe custody of such person during his pleasure in such place and in such manner as he deemed fit. The provisions of the section were to have retrospective effect. However, it is interesting that even prior to the Act of 1800 in *R. v. Ann Sturgeon*[12] the Old Bailey did not feel inhibited from ordering Ann Sturgeon to be sent directly to Bedlam, on finding her to be a lunatic. She had been indicted for stealing a brass saucepan, a pair of breeches and various other items.

Similarly under section 2 those who were found by a jury to be insane on their arraignment could also be kept in custody during his Majesty's pleasure. Under section 3, those who were apprehended in circumstances which "denote a derangement of mind and a purpose of committing some crime, for which if committed by a justice of the peace as a dangerous person suspected of being insane. Such person could not then be released on bail except by two justices, one being the justice who issued the warrant, or by the Quarter Sessions or by one of the judges of his Majesty's courts in Westminster Hall or by the Lord Chancellor.

Under section 4 the Privy Council or a Secretary of State could cause persons appearing to be insane and endeavouring to gain admittance to his Majesty to be kept in custody until the insanity of such person was inquired into. If found insane he could not be released until he recovered his sanity.

## 3. Insane Prisoners Act 1840

Section 1 of the Insane Prisoners Act 1840 empowered the Secretary of State to transfer by warrant to a lunatic asylum anyone in prison, whether sentenced or not, on the certificate of two justices of the peace, assisted by two physicians or surgeons, that he was insane. If the two physicians or surgeons certified that he had become of sound mind again, the Secretary of State could transfer him back to prison, or if his sentence had expired, discharge him. These provisions are remarkably like the Secretary of State's powers of transfer in sections 46, 47 and 48 of the Mental Health Act 1983 and no doubt are their origin.

Section 3 of the 1840 Act extended the provisions of the Criminal Lunatics Act 1800, which related to treason, murder or felony, to those charged with misdemeanours as well.

## 4. McNaghten's Case

The McNaghten Rules were not so much of a landmark as a convenient opportunity for the statement, by the judges, of what had been the common law position since 1800, in the context of *McNaghten's Case*.[13] In that case Daniel McNaghten was indicted at the Central Criminal Court for the murder of Edward Drummond by shooting him in the back.

Tindal L.C.J. said in his summing up that the question to be determined was whether at the time the act in question was committed, the prisoner had or had not the use of his understanding so as to know that he was doing a wrong or wicked act. If the jurors should be of the opinion that the prisoner was not sensible, at the time he committed it, that he was violating the laws both of God and man, then he would be entitled to a verdict in his favour; but if, on the contrary, they were of the opinion that when he committed the act he was in a sound state of mind, then their verdict must be against him. The jury returned a verdict of Not Guilty on the ground of insanity.

The verdict was debated in the House of Lords.[14] The House decided to ask the opinion of the Judges on the law governing insanity. When on the 19th June 1843 the Judges attended the House of Lords, five questions were put to them.

Maule J. felt unable to answer the questions because they had not arisen out of a particular case and because he had heard no arguments on them at the bar of the House of Lords or elsewhere. Further because any answers given by the Judges could embarrass the administration of justice if the answers were cited at criminal trials.

The rest of the Judges had no such compunction and Lord Chief Justice Tindal gave their unanimous opinion on the five questions as follows.

On the first question, regarding insane delusions in respect of one or more particular subjects or persons, the answer was that where persons labour under partial delusions only, and are not in other respects insane, notwithstanding that the party accused did the act complained of under the influence of an insane delusion, he is nevertheless punishable according to the nature of the crime committed, if he knew at the time of committing such crime that he was acting contrary to the law of the land.

The second and third questions, relating to the proper questions to be put to the jury and in what terms the question as to the prisoner's state of mind would be put to the jury, were answered together. The jurors should be told in all cases that every man is presumed to be sane and to possess a sufficient degree of reason to be responsible for his crimes, until the contrary be proved to their satisfaction; and that to establish a defence on the ground of insanity, it must be clearly proved that at the time of the committing of the act, the party accused was labouring under such defect of reason, from disease of the mind, as not to know the nature and quality of the act he was doing; or if he did know it, that he did not know he was doing what was wrong. The usual mode of putting the latter part of the question to the jury had been whether he knew the difference between right and wrong.

On the fourth question, regarding an insane delusion as to existing facts, the answer was that whether he was excused would depend on the nature of the delusion. Assuming that he labours under a partial delusion only, and is not in other respects insane, he should be considered in the same situation as to responsibility as if the facts were real. For example, if the delusion was that someone was attempting to take away his life and he kills that man, as he supposes in self-defence, he would be exempt from punishment. If the delusion was that the deceased had slandered him and he killed him in revenge, he would be liable to punishment.

The fifth question, related to a medical man, who had experience in dealing with insanity, but who had never examined the prisoner, being asked his opinion on the state of the prisoner's mind at the time he committed the act. The answer was that it would not be proper for such a medical man to give his opinion solely on the basis of what he had heard in court. It was for the jury to determine the truth of the facts deposed to. However, where the facts were admitted or not disputed and the question was substantially one of science only, the question could be put in a general form but it could not be insisted upon as of right.

The Lord Chancellor accepted that the House of Lords had the right to ask for the opinion of the Judges on abstract questions of existing law. He expressed his gratitude to the Judges.

Thus the answers of the judges in *McNaghten's Case* were given extra-judicially. The Judges did not consider them binding and there was quite a bit of criticism at the time.

Alderson B. criticised one of the answers, for instance, in *R. v. Frances*.[15] In that case, the prisoner was indicted for wilful murder. The defence was that the prisoner, at the time he committed the act which caused the death, was in a state of insanity. Witnesses were called on the part of the prisoner to show that insanity had existed in many members of the prisoner's family, and that he himself had been insane for the previous three years. A physician who had been in court during the whole trial was then called on the part of the prosecution and asked whether, having regard to the whole evidence, he was of the opinion that the prisoner, at the time he committed the alleged act was of unsound mind. Alderson B. held that such a question should not be put notwithstanding the opinion of the Judges in *McNaghten's Case*.

The answer of the Judges to the House of Lords on this question was: "We think the medical man, under the circumstances supposed can not in strictness be asked his opinion in the terms above stated, because each of those questions involves the determination of the truth of the facts deposed to, which it is for the jury to decide and the questions are not mere questions, upon a matter of science, in which case such evidence is inadmissible; but where the facts were admitted, or not disputed, and the question becomes substantially one of science only, it may be convenient to allow the question to be put in that general form, though the same can not be insisted on as a matter of right."

Alderson B. said that he was quite sure that the opinion was wrong and that the question should not be put at all. He held that the proper mode was to ask what are the symptoms of insanity, or to take particular facts and assuming them to be true, to ask whether they indicate insanity on the part of the prisoner. To take the course suggested, by the judges in answer to the House of Lords, was really to substitute the witness for the jury, and allow him to decide upon the whole case. The jury have the facts before them, and they alone must interpret them by the general opinions of scientific men. The prisoner was acquitted.

It must obviously be right that medical evidence must be limited to technical medical matters and should not extend to questions of fact which can be determined just as well by the jury. Unfortunately in modern times the judges allow medical men too much latitude and allow them to encroach on matters which should be left to the jury.[16]

Nevertheless *McNaghten's Case* has been followed for years and is still applied today. Remarks such as those of Lord Diplock about the vagaries of psychiatrists and the permanence of the McNaghten Rules in *R. v. Sullivan*[17] show how attached to the Rules the judges still are. The Rules were especially useful prior to 1907 because, as insanity is a question of fact, there was no legal authority on the subject other than the summing up of judges in cases like *R. v. Leyton*[18] and *R. v. Dixon*,[19] until the enactment of the Criminal Appeal Act 1907.

### 5. Trial of Lunatics Act 1883

The next change came in the Trial of Lunatics Act 1883, which amended the form of the special verdict to read "guilty but insane." This was thought to be a retrogressive step and was severely criticised, for instance by the Gowers Commission.[20] It was changed back to its original form of "not guilty by reason of insanity" by the Criminal Procedure (Insanity) Act 1964.

## 6. Mentally ill offenders in prison

By 1889 it became obvious that something had to be done about the growing number of people being sent to prison who were clearly insane. The Prison Commissioners brought the problem to the attention of the Home Secretary who issued a circular to magistrates, advising them to obtain evidence as to the mental condition of the accused who were alleged to be insane.[21] He pointed out that while, where serious crimes were concerned, it may be necessary to commit for trial persons alleged to be insane so that the jury could decide the issue, in less serious cases it was always open to the magistrates to dismiss the charge and to deal with the accused as an ordinary lunatic, either by handing him over to the care of his friends, or sending him as a pauper lunatic to an asylum. Thus in the case of minor offences committed by insane offenders the charges were to be dismissed, and instead of conviction or committal for trial, the offender was to be dealt with as an ordinary lunatic.

The Home Secretary's circular had more to do with alleviating the immense pressure on prisons than with providing better care for offenders who were insane. Thus this change occurred due to simple administrative expediency. Magistrates were already in the habit of dismissing very minor offences altogether in any case. This practice was envisaged by the Summary Jurisdiction Act 1879. Out of this in gradual stages, developed the Probation of Offenders Act 1907. That Act made clear that the mental condition of the accused would be one of the considerations which would justify the dismissal of the charge or the discharge of the accused on recognisances.

The final step was taken by the Mental Deficiency Act 1913. That Act was based on the Report of Lord Radnor's Royal Commission on the Care and Control of the Feeble-Minded (Cmnd. 4202). The Report recognised that there should be an improved system of institutions and guardianship which would not only protect the community against the mental defective but also protect him from abuse and exploitation by the community.

## 7. Mental Deficiency Act 1913

The main features of the 1913 Act were that the court, which convicted a mental defective of an offence for which he could be sent to prison, had the option of postponing the sentence and directing that civil committal proceedings be instituted for committing him to an institution or into guardianship. A summary court could do so without convicting him. Secondly, the court could either act on evidence given at the trial or call further medical or other evidence. Thirdly, pending committal the court could order him to be kept in an institution for mental defectives or in a "place of safety."

The 1913 Act had followed the Radnor Report's definition of mental deficiency, which excluded not only unsoundness of mind but also any defect of intelligence which had not been present from an early age. The Mental Deficiency Act 1927 widened the definition to include disorders which had been present before the age of eighteen. But even the 1927 Act left the main defect of the 1913 Act untouched. This was that, as suggested by the Radnor Report, it dealt with mental defect but not disorder. Thus the Act did not apply to those who became mentally ill later in life and committed offences. This defect was not put right until the passing of the Criminal Justice Act 1948. That Act provided that a summary court, trying a case involving an imprisonable offence, could commit the accused to a mental institution, if it was satisfied that the accused had committed the offence charged and that he was of unsound mind and also that he was "a proper person to be detained."

## 8. Criminal Justice Act 1948

This Act introduced a long overdue reform which had been delayed probably due to the war. It extended the application of probation provisions to mentally disordered offenders. The Probation of Offenders Act 1907 already referred to the mental condition of the offender in the making of a probation order. Section 4 provided that, on being satisfied, on adequate medical evidence, that the mental condition of the offender required and was susceptible to treatment, but not such as to justify certification under the Lunacy Act 1890 or the Mental Deficiency Act 1913, the court could make a probation order requiring the offender to submit to treatment for up to 12 months.

Thus the use of probation was made a means of ensuring treatment. Section 4 of the 1948 Act defined the circumstances in which a court could include in a probation order a requirement that the offender should undergo treatment "with a view to the improvement of his mental condition." These circumstances were that there had to be evidence by a "duly qualified medical practitioner appearing to the court to be experienced in the diagnosis of mental disorders''; the evidence had to be to the effect that the mental condition required, and was susceptible to, treatment but not such as to justify certification under the Lunacy or Mental Deficiency Acts; the court had to be satisfied that arrangements had been made or would be made for treatment, which had to be carried out by or under the direction of a duly qualified medical practitioner; the offender had to consent to the treatment and the submission of a report of his mental condition but his consent would not involve consent to any surgical or electrical treatment.

Section 24 of the 1948 Act empowered magistrates' courts to make reception orders for the reception and detention of the offender in an institution for persons of unsound mind if the court was satisfied that the person did that act or made the omission charged; that he was of unsound mind on the evidence of two duly qualified medical practitioners and that he was a proper person to be detained.

Finally, the probation order had to specify the period of treatment, which could not be for more than a year. Murder and other crimes carrying a fixed penalty of death were outside section 4. Strictly speaking, the offender was a voluntary patient but since he would be guilty of a breach of the order if he discontinued his treatment, there was some compulsion for him to continue with his treatment. This power is now to be found in section 3 of, and Schedule 1 to, the Powers of Criminal Courts Act 1973.

In-patient probation orders fell in number after the Mental Health Act 1959 introduced hospital orders but out-patient probation orders have been steadily increasing. The Homicide Act 1957 made provision for the defence of diminished responsibility in murder cases. The defence is discussed in Chapter 3.

## 9. The Mental Health Act 1959

The most substantial reform of the law relating to mentally disordered persons in general, and mentally disordered offenders in particular, was introduced by the 1959 Act. It was without doubt one of the most important pieces of social legislation this century.

The main effect of the 1959 Act was to bring up to date the law relating to mental disorder in one comprehensive code. Clearly the provisions of the Lunacy Act 1890 and the Mental Deficiency Acts 1913 and 1927, relating to certification, were no longer appropriate in the light of the National Health Service Act 1946, which provided for free hospital treatment for all. The Mental Treatment Act 1930, although it made provision for the voluntary treatment of patients without certification, was not wide enough to cover all types of mental disorder and was very cumbersome to operate. Further, advances had been made in the treatment of mental patients with modern drugs, which made them more manageable in ordinary hospitals. The 1959 Act took all these factors into account.

The Board of Control was abolished and its functions transferred to local authorities and Mental Health Review Tribunals, which were established under the Act to safeguard the interests of mental patients, who no longer needed to be certified. For the sake of completeness, to these the 1983 Act has added the Mental Health Act Commission as a further safeguard. Under the 1959 Act it was no longer necessary to send any patient to any particular type of hospital and the emphasis was on voluntary treatment as much as possible and the return of patients back to the community as soon as appropriate.

Only sections 60 to 80 in Part V of the 1959 Act are of direct interest to mental offenders. As explained above, prior to 1959 unless the mental offender came within the McNaghten Rules, or could plead diminished responsibility under section 2 of the Homicide Act 1957, he would be sent to prison although he was clearly suffering from mental disorder and treatment in hospital rather than a prison sentence was clearly appropriate. Imprisonment in these circumstances served neither the offender's interests nor the public interest; because without appropriate treatment in hospital the offender would be returned to the community, having served his sentence, without having been cured and in some cases probably even more mentally disordered than he was before he went to prison.

Another feature of the 1959 Act was the very wide definition of mental disorder in section 4(1) as "mental illness, arrested or incomplete development of mind, psychopathic disorder and any other disorder or disability of mind." Mental illness was left undefined, as it still is today, but incomplete development of mind was defined as "severe subnormality" and "subnormality." For the first time "psychopathic disorder" was defined as "persistent disorder or disability of mind (whether or not including subnormality of intelligence) which results in abnormally aggressive and seriously irresponsible conduct on the part of the patient, and requires or is susceptible to medical treatment."

So far as mentally disordered offenders were concerned, before a hospital order could be made the court had to be satisfied that the offender was suffering from mental illness, psychopathic disorder, subnormality or severe subnormality. No hospital order could be made if the patient suffered from "any other disorder or disability of mind." Any other disorder or disability of mind only applied to non-offender patients.

Further, section 97(1) of the 1959 Act[22] imposed a duty on the Minister of Health to provide such institutions as appear to him to be necessary, for persons subject to detention under the Act, who "in the opinion of the Minister," require treatment under conditions of special security on account of their dangerous violent or criminal propensities.

With the benefit of hindsight, it is clear that this duty leaves too much discretion to the Minister. As indeed its present equivalent in section 40 of the National Health Service Reorganisation Act 1973 also leaves too much discretion to the Minister. The minister is not in as good a position to determine whether conditions of special security are required as the court who tried the offender. The court would have seen the accused and his demeanour and heard all the evidence at first hand. Further, the court would not be diverted by considerations, such as the availability of adequate funding, which are not, strictly speaking, relevant to the question of whether treatment is required under conditions of special security in the case of a particular individual. It would have been far more satisfactory, therefore, at any rate so far as hospital orders are concerned, if the Minister were obliged to make provision for institutions for persons subject to detention under the 1983 Act who in the opinion of the court require treatment under conditions of special security, rather that leaving it to the discretion of the Minister to decide whether such treatment is required.[23]

Under section 60 of the 1959 Act courts of assize or quarter sessions (as they were called before the establishment of the Crown Court) could on convicting for an offence, the sentence for which was not fixed by law, make a hospital order if satisfied that certain conditions were met. These were firstly, that there was the written or oral evidence of two medical practitioners, at least one of whom was approved by a local authority under section 28 of the Act, that the offender was suffering from mental illness, psychopathic disorder, subnormality or severe subnormality. Secondly, that the mental disorder was of a nature or degree which warranted the detention of the offender in a hospital or his reception into guardianship. Thirdly, the court was of the opinion, having regard to all the circumstances, including the nature of the offence and the character and antecedents of the offender, and to the other available methods of dealing with him, that an order under section 60 was the most suitable way of disposing of the case.

Magistrates' courts, before making the order under section 60, had either to convict for an offence punishable on summary conviction with imprisonment or they had to be satisfied, on a charge for such an offence, that the accused did the act or made the omission in question without convicting him.

Before making a hospital order the court had to be satisfied that arrangements had been made for the admission of the offender to the hospital named in the order within 28 days or, in the case of a guardianship order, that the local authority, or any other person approved by that authority, was willing to receive the offender into guardianship. There was no requirement, as there is in section 37(4) of the Mental Health Act 1983, that the court should be satisfied only "on the written or oral evidence of the registered medical practitioner who would be in charge of his treatment or of some other person representing the managers of the hospital that arrangements have been made for his admission to that hospital..."

If in the view of the nature of the offence, the antecedents of the offender and the risk of repetition, it was thought that the offender should be subject to restrictions, courts, other than magistrates' courts, could make restriction orders under section 65, if necessary for the protection of the public. If a magistrates' court considered that a restriction order was appropriate, it could commit an offender of 14 or over to the quarter sessions under section 67. While the offender was awaiting the hearing of the quarter sessions, the offender could be detained in hospital as if he was under a restriction order.

During the period of a restriction order the patient could not be discharged, given leave of absence or transferred to another hospital without the consent of the Home Secretary. Section 66 gave sole power of discharge of such a patient to the Home Secretary. He could discharge the offender either absolutely or conditionally. A conditionally discharged patient was subject to recall by the Home Secretary during the period of the restriction order.

Once a restriction order ceased to have effect, either by the expiration of the period specified in the order or by a direction of the Home Secretary under section 66(1), the patient would be treated as though he had been admitted to hospital on a hospital order without restriction. That is, the patient and his nearest relative had the right to apply to a Mental Health Review Tribunal under section 63(4).

Thus Part V of the 1959 Act attempted to put offender patients as nearly as possible in the same position as non-offenders. The effect of a hospital order under section 60 or section 61 (which related to children and young persons) without restriction, was the same as a compulsory civil admission under Part IV, subject to two exceptions. The nearest relative had no power to discharge but could apply to a

Mental Health Review Tribunal under section 63(4) at annual intervals. Secondly, the automatic discharge of young non-offender patients suffering from psychopathic disorder or subnormality on reaching the age of 25, in the absence of an objection from the responsible medical officer on the ground that the patient would be dangerous to himself or to others, did not apply to an offender patient even though he may have been under 21 at the time the order was made. The offender patient nevertheless still had the same rights as non-offenders to apply to a Mental Health Review Tribunal at any time during the 6 months following the making of the order.

The differences between non-offender patients and restricted offender patients were even greater, as would be expected. Neither the restricted offender patient nor his nearest relative could apply to a Mental Health Review Tribunal. Only the Home Secretary could refer the case to a Tribunal for advice at any time and the patient could require him to do so under sections 66(6) and (7) at any time after a year from the making of the order. These patients could not be given leave of absence nor transferred to other hospitals or received into guardianship without the Home Secretary's consent. The responsible medical officer was required to keep under constant review the possibility of discharge of restricted patients. This was normally at the same intervals as other patients.

Under sections 71 to 79 of the 1959 Act, the Home Secretary could transfer patients from prisons, approved schools or remand homes to hospital or from remand homes into guardianship. Recommendations of two doctors would be needed, at least one of whom had to be approved under section 28, to satisfy the Home Secretary that the prisoner was suffering from mental illness, psychopathic disorder, subnormality or severe subnormality of a nature or degree which warranted his detention in hospital for medical treatment.

Further the Home Secretary had also to be of the opinion, having regard to the public interest, that in all the circumstances of the case the transfer was expedient. Although there was no requirement in section 72 for the Home Secretary to be satisfied that arrangements had been made for the admission of the prisoner to hospital, as there was in section 60(3), according to information given to the Butler Committee[24] the Home Secretary in practice sought the consent of the hospital before directing transfers from prison.

Usually the Home Secretary would not have made a transfer direction within a week of the prisoner's earliest date of release nor would he have imposed restrictions. He would have arranged for the prisoner's admission to hospital after his release from prison.

The Butler Committee thought that the objections made to it by the National Council for Civil Liberties that a transfer direction would unnecessarily prolong a prison sentence were largely theoretical. For one reason they did not think that a hospital would accept the transfer of a prisoner who required not treatment but merely continued custodial detention. They did not therefore recommend any formal limitation on the timing of transfers.[25] Indeed no such limits were included in the Mental Health (Amendment) Act 1982. Instead they recommended that every transferred prisoner should have the right to apply to a Mental Health Review Tribunal at the time that his earliest date of release would have been reached. Similarly, at that time the Home Secretary should review the necessity of continuing restrictions, which may have been imposed, and if possible remove them.[26]

The Butler Committee also recommended that the powers conferred by section 72 should not be restricted to mental illness, psychopathic disorder, subnormality and severe subnormality but should be extended to all prisoners suffering from mental disorder. Unfortunately this recommendation has not been implemented. Section 47 of the Mental Health Act 1983 is still limited in the same way as in the 1959 Act.

The Mental Health (Amendment) Act 1982 made various changes to the Mental Health Act 1959. The Mental Health Act 1983 has consolidated these changes with the provisions of the 1959 Act. These Acts are considered in detail in later chapters.

CHAPTER 2:  DEFENCE OF INSANITY

## 1.  The defence at Common Law

At Common Law there was the ancient and humane principle "that if a person was at the time of his unlawful act mentally so disordered that it would be unreasonable to impute guilt to him, he ought not to be liable to conviction and punishment."[1]  It has always been for the accused to prove that he was insane at the time of the commission of the offence.[2]  This exception to the general principle that the burden of proving guilt in criminal cases is on the Crown was recognised by the House of Lords in *Woolmington v. D.P.P.*[3]  The accused need do no more than adduce evidence sufficient to satisfy the jury of the existence of the defence on a balance of probabilities.[4]

## 2.  Criminal Lunatics Act 1800

The defence was put on a statutory basis by the Criminal Lunatics Act 1800 as a result of the difficulties encountered in *R. v. Hadfield*.[5]  Hadfield had been charged with high treason in attempting to assassinate George III and acquitted "he being under the influence of insanity at the time the act was committed."  One of the difficulties was that of disposal.  As Lord Kenyon said:[6] "The prisoner for his own sake, and for the sake of society at large, must not be discharged."  He went on to say that "it is absolutely necessary for the safety of society, that he should be properly disposed of, all mercy and humanity being shown to this most unfortunate creature."  However, there was no means of making provision for the proper care of such a person "with all the attention and all the relief that can be afforded to him."

The Act of 1800 tried to overcome this difficulty by providing that where anyone was found to be "not guilty, on the ground of insanity"[7] it should be lawful for His Majesty to give such order for the safe custody of such person, during his pleasure, in such place and in such manner as His Majesty should deem fit.  Section 2 of the Act of 1800 made provision for defendants who appeared to the jury to be insane and unfit to plead; the jury could find them to be "insane on arraignment"[8] and the court could again proceed to order detention during His Majesty's pleasure.

## 3. The McNaghten Case

The next landmark was *the McNaghten Case*[9] which led to the House of Lords putting five questions to the judges concerning insanity. (See Chapter 1, section 4 above). Thus the principle was established that everyone is presumed to be sane and responsible for his actions. A further principle was laid down "that to establish a defence on the ground of insanity it must be clearly proved that at the time of committing the act the accused was labouring under such a defect of reason, from disease of mind, as not to know the nature and quality of the act he was doing, or, if he did know it, that he did not know he was doing what was wrong."

As stated by Tindal L.C.J. at the trial itself: "If he was not sensible at the time he committed that act, that it was a violation of the law of God and man, undoubtedly he is not responsible for that act or liable to any punishment whatever flowing from it."[10]

## 4. The Butler recommendations

Although some of the recommendations of the Butler Committee[11] have been implemented in the Mental Health Act 1983, nothing has been done about modernising the law on insanity and making it a workable and worthwhile defence. Thus the defence of insanity is raised in no more than two or three cases a year.[12] One of the reasons for the virtual disappearance of the defence of insanity is that judges still try to apply the antiquated McNaghten Rules.[13]

Apart from the actual complication of having to prove clearly that the defendant was labouring under a defect of reason, from disease of mind, so as not to know the nature and quality of the act he was doing or that he did not know it was wrong, the Rules are too narrow to provide a defence to some one who is clearly mentally disordered but has psychotic delusions.[14]

A psychotic illness was defined by the World Health Organisation in 1978 as meaning a disorder "in which the impairment of mental function has developed to a degree that interferes grossly with insight, ability to meet some ordinary demands of life or to maintain adequate contact with reality." This definition clearly covers those with an "abnormality of mind" as defined by Lord Parker in *R. v. Byrne*[15] in the context of section 2(1) of the Homicide Act 1957. (See Chapter 3, section 7). Those with psychotic delusions would also be covered by the definition of severe mental illness proposed by the Butler Committee, set out in the following pages.

Another difficulty with the insanity defence is that the matter has to go to the jury, whereas in the case of diminished responsibility cases under section 2 of the Homicide Act 1957, the judge can accept a plea. In fact about 80 per cent of diminished responsibility cases do not go to the jury. It may be justifiable that the defence of insanity should always be a matter for the jury as it is technically an acquittal. Nevertheless it is a factor which discourages defendants from raising the insanity defence and relying instead on the defence of diminished responsibility.

Previously a major difficulty with the defence of insanity was the inflexibility of sentencing. On acquittal on the grounds of insanity under section 5(1) of the Criminal Procedure (Insanity) Act 1964, the defendant had to be sent to a hospital specified by the Home Secretary. He was then treated, by virtue of paragraph 2(1) of Schedule 1 to the 1964 Act, as if a hospital order, together with a restriction order without a limitation of time had been made. If on the other hand, instead of seeking acquittal on the grounds of insanity, the defendant had pleaded guilty to manslaughter, on the grounds of diminished responsibility, then his sentence could have been as lenient as a probation order, where that was all that the circumstances warranted. This anomaly has now been put right by the Criminal Procedure (Insanity and Unfitness to Plead) Act 1991.

The Butler Committee had recognised the unsatisfactory state of the law as laid down in the Criminal Procedure (Insanity) Act 1964. This unsatisfactory state of the law was highlighted by the, House of Lords in the case of *R. v. Sullivan*;[16] and more recently by the Court of Appeal in *R. v. Burgess*.[17] (See following section of this Chapter). The Butler Committee had made proposals to remedy the situation, relating to defendants who were mentally disordered at the time they committed the offence and defendants who were so disordered at the time of trial. It does not inspire confidence in the speed at which such reforms are implemented, when it has not been possible to implement these thoroughly sensible provisions until the enactment of the Criminal Procedure (Insanity and Unfitness to Plead) Act 1991.

The 1991 Act made two principal changes to the law of insanity. One is that the Court will be able to examine the facts of the case to see if the defendant committed the actus reus of the offence, even after it has determined that the defendant is unfit to plead. This is an improvement on the Butler proposal, which was not limited to the actus reus. Clearly once the Court has found that the defendant is unfit to plead it would be meaningless to enquire into the state of his mind relating to his intentions. The second principal change is that the Court is no longer required to make a hospital order if the defendant is unfit to plead or not guilty by reason of insanity. A defendant found unfit to plead but not proved to have committed the offence on the examination of the facts, will be acquitted. Where the offence is proved, except where the sentence is mandatory (i.e. murder and treason), the Court will have the option of making hospital orders, with or without restrictions, or discharge the defendant, or to make any other suitable order, such as guardianship or a psychiatric probation order under Schedule 1A of the Powers of Criminal Courts Act 1973, as introduced by the Criminal Justice Act 1991, Schedule 1, part II, paragraph 5.

In order to obviate the difficulties in proving insanity under the McNaghten Rules, the Butler Committee suggested that the Rules should be abolished and replaced by a verdict of "not guilty by reason of mental disorder." This suggestion has still not been implemented. The Butler Committee defined ''mental disorder'' as severe mental impairment under the Mental Health Act 1983 (in 1975, of course, it was severe subnormality under the 1959 Act) or severe mental illness which paragraph 18.35 of the Butler Report suggested should be mental illness with "one or more of the following characteristics:-

(a) lasting impairment of intellectual functions shown by failure of memory, orientation, comprehension and learning capacity;

(b) lasting alteration of mood of such degree as to give rise to delusional appraisal of the patient's situation, his past or his future, or that of others, or to lack of any appraisal;

(c) delusional beliefs, persecutory, jealous or grandiose;

(d) abnormal perceptions associated with delusional misinterpretation of events;

(e) thinking so disordered as to prevent reasonable appraisal of the patient's situation or reasonable communication with others."

The Butler Committee's suggested definition goes much wider than the McNaghten Rules. As the Report says in paragraph 18.36, it draws the line of criminal responsibility at a place and in a way to which medical witnesses can testify.

## 5. Comparison of the insanity defence with automatism and intoxication defences

When the defence of insanity is looked at together with the defences of automatism and intoxication, it is difficult to determine precisely what the logic or justification is behind the decisions on these defences. There does not appear to be a logical thread running through them. The recent cases of *R. v. Bailey*[18] and *R. v. Sullivan* go some way towards clarifying the position but even they are not entirely consistent, as explained below.

To deal with the defences of insanity, automatism and intoxication in a logical way, one would need to determine whether the basis of these defences should be that of criminal responsibility or simply the protection of society, whether the accused can be said to be responsible in any meaningful way or not. The decided cases avoid this question.

If the basis of these defences is a question of responsibility, then it is difficult to see how any one can be responsible for an act he is not conscious of performing. If, on the other hand, the basis is protecting society by deterring the particular type of behaviour, it again fails. As the accused is not aware of what he is doing, how can he be discouraged from repeating it? Although it could be argued that others might be deterred by the fact that the possibility of punishment exists even when these defences are pleaded. Thus it would appear that the perceived deterrent effect and the consequent protection of the public predominates in these cases and other principles give way to it.

In trying to find a logical basis for the defences of insanity, automatism and intoxication, one must accept that the basis of these defences, whatever it is, cannot be simply the lack of guilty intention. If that was all that the defences amounted to, they would not be necessary at all except in cases of strict liability. The defences must therefore be something more than simply the lack of "mens rea."

## 6. The defence of automatism

In order for the defendant to be guilty of a crime it must be proved that he voluntarily committed the act in question. If the movement of his limbs was involuntary in that it did not flow from an exercise of the defendant's will because he was unconscious at the time or in a state of hypoglycaemia, then the defence of automatism will be available to him. This is illustrated by cases like *R. v. Quick*[19] and *R. v. Bailey*. The only material difference between them was that the latter was convicted of a crime of specific intent, that is, wounding with intent to cause grievous bodily harm contrary to section 18 of the Offences Against the Person Act 1861. Bailey had also been charged in the alternative of unlawful wounding contrary to section 20 of that Act. The jury were not, however, required to return a verdict on the alternative count.

Both *Quick* and *Bailey* were diabetics claiming that when they committed the alleged assaults they were in a state of hypoglycaemia through an imbalance between their intake of insulin and food. The judge in *R. v. Bailey* had failed to distinguish between crimes of specific intent and basic intent. The Court of Appeal held that this was wrong. Even if the automatism was self-induced, it could still be a defence to a crime of specific intent. To decide otherwise would be to put a self-induced automaton in a worse position than a self-induced drunkard. Thus whereas a drunkard has no defence to a crime of basic intent the automaton may have.

The reasoning of the Court was that an intoxicated person has no defence to a crime of basic intent because the conduct of the accused is reckless and recklessness is enough to constitute the, necessary "mens rea" in assault cases where specific intent does not form part of the charge. The same, however, cannot be said in the cases of other forms of self-induced automatism because while it is common knowledge that those who take alcohol may become aggressive, it is not common knowledge that those who fail to take food after an insulin injection may also be aggressive. Thus in each case the prosecution must prove recklessness.

Griffiths L.J. said in *R. v. Bailey*[20] in the case of assault, if the accused knows that his action or inaction is likely to make him aggressive, unpredictable or uncontrolled, with the result that he may cause injury to others and he persists in the action he takes or takes no remedial action when he knows that it is required, it will be open to the jury to find that he was reckless."

In *R. v. Bailey* Griffiths L.J. went on to say that "the Recorder never invited the jury to consider what the appellant's knowledge or appreciation was of what would happen if he failed to take food after his insulin or whether he realised that he might become aggressive. Nor were they asked to consider why the appellant had omitted to take food · in time. They were given no direction on the elements of recklessness. Accordingly, in our judgement there was also a misdirection in relation to the second count in the indictment of unlawful wounding." Nevertheless the court went on to hold that even if the jury had been properly directed they must have rejected the appellant's defence. Consequently as no miscarriage of justice had occurred in spite of the misdirection's, the appeal was dismissed.

## 7. The test of recklessness

*R. v. Bailey* seems to ignore the decision of the House of Lords in *R. v. Caldwell*.[21] In that case the defendant set fire to a residential hotel where he had been employed. He was so drunk at the time that it did not occur to him that there might be people there whose lives may be endangered. The jury were directed that self-induced drunkenness was no defence to the charge under section 1(2) of the Criminal Damage Act 1971, that is intending to damage property, intending to endanger life or being reckless as to whether life was endangered or not. The Court of Appeal quashed the conviction under that subsection. On appeal to the House of Lords, it was held that if the charge had been only concerned with the intent to endanger life, self-induced drunkenness could be relevant as a defence, but not when the charge included a reference to being reckless as to whether life would be endangered. Classification of offences into "specific" or "basic" intent was irrelevant where being reckless as to whether a particular harmful effect will result from one's act was sufficient alternative to "mens rea."[22]

*R. v. Bailey* instead of following this concept of what amounts to recklessness goes back to assuming that recklessness involves a subjective awareness of risk. In any case, is recklessness meaningful in this context, where we are not talking about recklessness which accompanies the act constituting the offence but recklessness which goes back several stages? Is recklessness as to what one did or did not have for breakfast relevant to what happened after dinner? This concept of recklessness seems artificial in the context of these defences.

It is of course just possible that the learned Recorder in *R. v. Bailey* did not take *R. v. Caldwell* into consideration because he thought that the test laid down in *R. v. Cunningham*[23] was the relevant criterion. In that case the appellant had been charged under section 23 of the Offences Against the Person Act 1861 that he unlawfully and maliciously caused to be taken by Sarah Wade a noxious thing thereby endangering her life.

The Court of Criminal Appeal held that the trial judge had been wrong to direct the jury that it was not necessary to prove that Roy

Cunningham had intended to poison the old lady. It was enough that he had done it unlawfully and maliciously. The judge interpreted malicious as meaning no more than wicked. Byrne J. in a unanimous judgement said: "In our view it should have been left to the jury to decide whether, even if the appellant did not intend the injury to Mrs. Wade, he foresaw that the removal of the gas meter might cause injury to someone but nevertheless removed it."

*W. (a minor) v. Dolbey*[24] follows *R. v. Cunningham*. In *Dolbey* the defendant was charged with unlawfully and maliciously wounding R. contrary to section 20 of the Offences Against the Person Act 1861. The justices found that the defendant had been reckless, and that was sufficient to constitute the malicious intent required by the 1861 Act. On appeal to the Divisional Court, it was held, allowing the appeal and quashing the conviction, that in order to establish that a defendant had acted maliciously it had to be shown that on the facts known to him at the time, he actually foresaw that a particular kind of harm might be done to his victim. Accordingly if the defendant honestly believed that the gun was not loaded then, whether or not he was reckless in pointing it at someone without first checking it, he did not foresee the physical harm done to R. and therefore he was not malicious.

Another relevant case is *R. v. Hardie*[25]. The defendant lived with a woman in her flat. He became upset and took several tablets of valium. He had no knowledge of the effect the tablets might have. Later he started a fire thereby endangering the lives of the woman and her daughter. The judge directed the jury that a self-administered drug could not negate "mens rea." He was convicted under section 1(2) of the Criminal Damage Act 1971. On appeal, it was held that the jury should have been directed that if they came to the conclusion that at the time the defendant was unable to appreciate the risks to property and persons from his actions they should then consider whether the taking of the valium had itself been reckless. Thus the appeal was allowed.

In *R. v. Sullivan* the appellant had kicked a man violently while suffering from a seizure due to psychomotor epilepsy. The evidence was that the appellant would have made automatic movements of which he was not conscious. The judge ruled that the jury could not find the appellant not guilty because of automatism but that the proper verdict was not guilty by reason of insanity. Thereupon the appellant changed his plea to guilty of assault occasioning actual bodily harm and was convicted accordingly. The House of Lords held that despite a reluctance to attach a label of insanity to a sufferer from epilepsy, the special verdict would have been the proper one. Lord Diplock said:[26] "If the effect of a disease is to impair these faculties so severely as to have either of the consequences referred to in the latter part of the [McNaghten] rules, it matters not whether the aetiology of the impairment itself is permanent or transient and intermittent, provided that it subsisted at the time of the commission of the act. The purpose of the legislation relating to the defence of insanity ever since 1800, has been to protect society against recurrence of the dangerous conduct."

In *R. v. Burgess*[27] it was decided, following *R. v. Sullivan*, that violence occurring when the appellant was sleep-walking amounted to insanity under the McNaghten Rules and was not automatism. The reason being, here again that the cause of the violence was not external. The appellant admitted that he had attacked Katrina Curtis by hitting her on the head whereby she sustained laceration of her scalp which needed stitches. Miss Curtis was a neighbour with whom the appellant used to watch video tapes. On the occasion in question they had fallen asleep. When he woke up he realised he was holding Miss Curtis down on the floor. He could not remember hitting her.

The Court of Appeal's reasoning was that sleep-walking was an abnormality of the brain function and was therefore a pathological condition. Further, it could recur although there was no record of anyone being prosecuted twice for a sleep-walking offence. Sleep walking was treatable, it therefore made sense to detain the appellant in hospital.

*R. v. Burgess* appears to go further than *R. v. Sullivan* because in the latter case it was the epileptic fit which caused the appellant's mental difficulty; in the former case it was sleep, which cannot be said to be an abnormality like epilepsy.

In *R. v. Quick* the defendant was a diabetic and he relied on the defence of automatism to a charge of assaulting a patient at the hospital where he was working as a nurse. It was held by the Court of Appeal that "disease of mind" within the meaning of the McNaghten Rules was a malfunctioning of the mind caused by disease and did not include malfunctioning of the mind due to a transitory effect caused by the application to the body of some external factor, such as insulin, and therefore the facts did not support a verdict of insanity. Accordingly the defence of automatism should have been left to the jury.

Thus the essence of the distinction which allows the diabetic to escape the label of insanity is that the cause of the automatic state is external, and not internal or organic. The hypoglycaemia coma was caused by the use of insulin and not by the diabetes itself. However, this is not entirely consistent as there could be instances where the pancreas overproduces insulin and thus the automatic state would be internal. It is difficult to see how in that case the person suffering from hypoglycaemia would not be insane within the McNaghten Rules; since as decided in *R. v. Kemp*[28] "disease of mind" in the Rules means a disease which affects the mind. It would therefore include a disease of the pancreas which may produce too much insulin leading to hypoglycaemia. It would be utterly illogical to make a distinction between the two types of diabetic and call one insane and not the other; but that is where the decided cases would drive us to.

As stated above, these cases reflect a failure to determine the proper basis of the defence of insanity. Is it an excuse for the offence? That is, that as the person is incapable of practical reasoning, he is not susceptible to the deterrents provided by law. He is therefore excused as there is no point in punishing him.

## 8. Defences as mitigating factors

Few would argue that mental disorder, automatism or intoxication have no relevance to a criminal trial. It may be, however, that these defences should be relegated from defences to simply mitigating factors on the ground of lesser moral fault. This would of course need primary legislation. As shown by Lord Diplock's remark in *R. v. Sullivan* about the vagaries of psychiatrists and the permanence of the McNaghten Rules, the judges are still wedded to the McNaghten Rules even after a century and a half and are not likely to change them in the interests of logical thought unless they are obliged to do so by new legislation on the subject.

## 9. Unfitness to plead

The question of whether a person is unfit to plead is usually determined when the accused is arraigned; but it can be raised at any time by the prosecution, defence or the court. Under section 4 of the Criminal Procedure (Insanity) Act 1964 (as substituted by section (2) of the Criminal Procedure (Insanity and Unfitness to Plead) Act 1991) where the question arises whether the accused is under a disability which would be a bar to his being tried, the court may have regard to the nature of the supposed disability and may postpone the question of fitness to plead until any time upto the opening of the defence.

If the jury return a verdict of not guilty the question of the accused's fitness to plead does not have to be decided. This is illustrated by *R. v. Burles*[29] where the appellant was charged with manslaughter of a fellow patient in a mental hospital. The medical evidence was that he could not understand spoken language and his ability to communicate intelligently was restricted. It was held that it was expedient to postpone the trial of the issue of fitness to plead, whatever the degree and nature of his disability, because the near certainty that the prosecution would have been unable to prove its case was a primary consideration under section 4(2) of the 1964 Act.

*R. v. Robertson*[30] decided that where the question of unfitness to plead was raised by the Crown, the onus of proof was on the Crown and the standard of proof was the ordinary standard in criminal cases, that is, proof beyond a reasonable doubt. Otherwise, the question of unfitness to plead is determined on the balance of probabilities.

Under section 4(5) of the 1964 Act the question of fitness to be tried has to be determined by a jury. Where it falls to be determined on the arraignment of the accused and the trial proceeds, the accused has to be tried by a different jury, other than the one which determined fitness. Where fitness falls to be determined at any later time than the arraignment, it has to be determined either by a separate jury or by a jury by whom the accused is being tried, as the court may direct. The determination as to fitness has to be on the written or oral evidence of two or more registered medical practitioners at least one of whom is duly approved.

While the law tries to strike a balance between the interests of the public by protecting them from mentally disordered offenders, and the interests of the offender by trying to cure him and rehabilitate him, the interests of justice probably suffer in the process. Admittedly the mentally disordered offender is tried in open court and the rules of natural justice are upheld. Nevertheless the outdated McNaghten Rules produce cases like *R. v. Sullivan* with the approval of the House of Lords.

Further, often the period of detention of a person found not guilty by reason of insanity is not commensurate with the gravity of the offence he has committed. He could be the subject of a hospital order, with restrictions on his discharge, for a comparatively minor offence. The balance between the need to protect the public and to be fair to a mentally disordered person, who may have committed only a minor offence, needs far more consideration with a view to changing the balance in favour of the mentally disordered offender.

## CHAPTER 3: THE DEFENCE OF DIMINISHED RESPONSIBILITY

### 1. Introduction of defence

The defence of diminished responsibility was introduced in Scotland about the middle of the nineteenth century by judges who wanted to avoid the mandatory consequences of a finding of murder, where the accused was not insane but nevertheless not fully responsible for his actions.[1] Thus while the accused was still culpable he could be found guilty of a lesser offence and sent to prison instead of being hanged.

The defence was introduced in England and Wales by the Homicide Act 1957 for the same reason. It is worth recalling that at the time there were two types of murder. Capital murder, that is killing such as by shooting or in furtherance of theft, which carried a mandatory death sentence, and non-capital murder, which included other unlawful killings and did not lead to the death sentence.

In this context section 2(1) of the 1957 Act provided that where a person killed or was a party to the killing of another he would not be convicted of murder if he was suffering from such abnormality of mind as substantially impaired his mental responsibility for his acts and omissions in doing or being a party to the killing. It was immaterial whether the abnormality arose from a condition of arrested or retarded development of mind or any inherent causes or induced by disease or injury.

Under section 2(2) of the 1957 Act it is for the defence to raise the issue of diminished responsibility and to prove that the accused is not liable to a conviction of murder by virtue of the section. If the defence is successful, the accused is found guilty of manslaughter and not murder. With the effective abolition of the death penalty since 1965, the main reason for the defence has gone. Nevertheless it provides flexibility as a finding of murder still carries a mandatory life sentence. Thus it brings a successful plea of diminished responsibility within the hospital order provisions of the Mental Health Act 1983. The judge has no choice but to impose a sentence of life imprisonment if the defendant is found guilty of murder. But if the offence is reduced to manslaughter due to diminished responsibility, then the judge does have a wide choice of sentences, including a hospital order if he thinks that it is the most suitable way of disposing of the case.

## 2. Judge or jury

*R. v. Matheson*[2] had decided that the question of whether the defendant was suffering from such abnormality of mind, as to substantially impair his responsibility, so as to reduce the murder to manslaughter, was one for the jury. Even if the prosecution agreed that the defendant's responsibility was impaired and offered no evidence to contradict this.

As explained by Lawton L.J. in *R. v. Vinagre*,[3] there were distressing cases where distraught defendants, mostly women, had to sit in the dock listening to hours of evidence of what they had done when they were in a state of mental imbalance. It was thought that it was wrong to subject such defendants to this additional ordeal, when it was agreed by the prosecution that, from the available medical reports, it was obvious that the defendant clearly suffered from diminished responsibility. As a result, in 1962 the judges decided that pleas of manslaughter on grounds of diminished responsibility could be accepted without the necessity of a jury trial.

As Scarman L. J. had pointed out in *R. v. Ford*[4], cases are tried by the courts and not by psychiatrists. It was for the judge to decide whether to accept a plea to manslaughter on the grounds of diminished responsibility; but he could accept such a plea only when there was clear evidence of mental imbalance. In *Vinagre's Case*, Orlando Vinagre had stabbed his wife in a frenzy when he was suffering from what the psychiatrists referred to in picturesque language as the "Othello syndrome." This was defined as being "morbid jealousy for which there was no cause." The defendant's wife had been going out with a policeman called Mick. The question was whether she was being unfaithful to her husband by having a sexual relationship with Mick. If there was no liaison then the possibility of the Othello syndrome would arise. On the other hand, if there was evidence that the wife had been unfaithful, then it would be difficult to offer the same psychiatric defence. Park J. had accepted a plea of manslaughter and the appeal turned on whether a life sentence was wrong in the circumstances. The Court of Appeal substituted seven years' imprisonment.

*R. v. Cox*[5] was the first case where the Court of Appeal confirmed that a plea of manslaughter, on the grounds of diminished responsibility, could be accepted by the judge and did not have to be left to the jury when there was no dispute as to the defendant's abnormality of mind. Where the medical evidence plainly pointed to substantially diminished responsibility, it was perfectly proper to accept a plea of guilty to manslaughter based on that ground. Winn L.J. criticised the fact that the matter had been left to the jury "as a result of which time and money was spent and the appellant no doubt kept in some anxiety and uncertainty whilst the trial went on." The sentence of life imprisonment for manslaughter based on substantially diminished responsibility was varied to one of a hospital order coupled with an indefinite restriction order, as a safe hospital was available for the detention of the appellant.

## 3. Defence to prove diminished responsibility

In *R. v. Ahmed Din*[6] it was held that it was the duty of the prosecution to prove the question whether the defendant's beliefs were due to a delusion or not. As in *Vinagre's Case*, the defendant thought that his wife was being unfaithful to him. The defence of diminished responsibility was based on an abnormality of mind resulting from paranoia due to a belief in his wife's infidelity for which there was no reasonable ground. However, there was no evidence to suggest that the defendant's belief was unreasonable and the prosecution had cross-examined the doctors only with a view to eliminating the question of insanity.

Stable J. left it to the jury to decide whether they were satisfied that, on balance of probabilities, the defendant's beliefs were delusional and that he had no ground for suspecting his wife's infidelity. The Court of Criminal Appeal pointed out that whether the defendant had solid grounds for believing in his wife's infidelity was not a matter for doctors. They could have views on it but their views were no better evidence than any other views. It was not a medical question. The defence had to prove the facts upon which the doctors could express their opinions as experts. Instead the defence relied on hearsay evidence of the doctors. At the same time, if the prosecution had considered step by step the ingredients of the defence, it would be apparent that it was its duty to probe the question whether or not the defendant was suffering from a delusion. The Court refused to interfere with the conviction of non-capital murder.

In *Walton v. R.*[7] the Privy Council reached a similar conclusion. Where an issue of diminished responsibility was raised on a charge of murder, the jury were entitled and bound to consider, not only the medical evidence, but also the evidence upon the whole facts and circumstances on whether the defence had been made out.

In another case, *R. v. Campbell*[8], the appellant had been charged with the murder of a young woman. He pleaded guilty to manslaughter by reason of provocation, but the prosecution refused to accept that plea. During the trial evidence was given by a psychiatrist as to the appellant's state of mind, to assist the jury on the issue of provocation. That evidence revealed mental abnormality but the question of whether that would have substantially impaired the appellant's responsibility for the killing was not considered, as the defence had not raised the issue of diminished responsibility. The appeal was on the question whether the judge should have directed the jury not only on provocation but also on diminished responsibility despite the fact that the latter defence had not been raised at the trial.

The Court of Appeal held that section 2(2) of the Homicide Act 1957 placed the burden of proving the defence of diminished responsibility on the defence. It had to be proved on a balance of probabilities. As the psychiatrist had never addressed the question as to whether the abnormality of the appellant's mind was such as substantially to impair responsibility for the killing there was not before the jury even "prima facie" evidence of the defence of diminished responsibility. Accordingly the judge was right to say that there was no evidence whatever to substantiate that defence.

The Court pointed out that, as decided in *R. v. Kooken*,[9] the defence of diminished responsibility under section 2(1) of the 1957 Act was an optional one, and, at least in cases where the defendant is represented by Counsel, the most that a trial judge should do, if he detects evidence of diminished responsibility, is to point out to defence counsel, in the absence of the jury, what he has detected, so that the defence can consider whether they regard the issue as one for the jury to decide.

## 4. Problem with timing of defence

A problem which arises for a mentally ill person charged with murder is that he cannot, like other defendants, deny the charge and then, if convicted, produce evidence as to his illness. A mentally ill person who denies that he has killed any one cannot wait until after the verdict before revealing that he is mentally disordered. For the defence of diminished responsibility he has to put his illness in issue before the jury.[10] The difficulty is that he needs to persuade the jury that he has no connection with the offence; but his credibility will be undermined if he has, at the same time, to persuade them that he is mentally disordered. If he says nothing about his mental illness before the verdict he cannot raise the issue of diminished responsibility after the verdict. Thus if the jury find against him, he will be convicted of murder and receive a mandatory sentence, no matter how mentally ill he is.

Exceptionally this problem was avoided in *R. v. Harvey*[11] as the only evidence against the accused was her own confession, which she retracted. She was therefore acquitted although there was evidence of diminished responsibility.

## 5. Success of the defence

It is extraordinary that ever since the defence of diminished responsibility was introduced, it has enjoyed a high success rate. In the first two years of operation it succeeded in over 70 per cent of the cases in which it was raised.[12] Some twenty years later in 1976 and 1977 the success rate was 90 per cent. What is more, in 80 per cent of cases in which the defence was raised, the defendant's plea to manslaughter was accepted and there was no trial.[13] In the two years 1976 and 1977 there was disagreement between doctors on the issue of diminished responsibility in no more than 13 per cent of the cases in which the defence was raised.[14]

## 6. Continuing need for the defence

Although the death penalty has been abolished and a system of hospital orders, with or without restrictions, introduced under the mental health legislation, there is still a need for the diminished responsibility defence. The Criminal Law Revision Committee advocated its retention even if the mandatory sentence of life imprisonment for murder were to be abolished.[15]

The Butler Committee, on the other hand, thought that the defence of diminished responsibility would not be needed if there were no mandatory sentence for murder.[16] The objection that its abolition would leave the stigma of an unqualified conviction of murder for people, who would otherwise receive a verdict of manslaughter, by reason of diminished responsibility, could be met, if on a charge for murder the jury were empowered to return a verdict of murder (or manslaughter) by reason of extenuating circumstances. Unlike the position in some American states, the extenuating circumstances would be left to be defined by law, as suggested by the Butler Committee.

It is remarkable that although the insanity defence leads to an acquittal, whereas the diminished responsibility defence does not, the defence of insanity has been almost entirely superseded by the latter defence. The reasons for this are not hard to find. It is not easy to bring a defendant within the outdated concepts of the McNaghten Rules.[17] Only the jury can decide the question of insanity; and until the Criminal procedure (Insanity and Unfitness to Plead) Act 1991, there was no flexibility in sentencing. The defendant had to be given a hospital order with restrictions and sent to a hospital specified by the Home Secretary.[18] Although section 6 of the Criminal Procedure (Insanity) Act 1964 provides that where diminished responsibility is raised by the defence, the prosecution may adduce evidence to prove insanity, this hardly ever happens.[19]

## 7. Circumstances when the defence is available

*R. v. Byrne*[20] defined abnormality of mind "as a state of mind so different from ordinary human beings that the reasonable man would term it abnormal. It appears to us to be wide enough to cover the mind's activities in all its aspects, not only the perception of physical acts and matters, and the ability to form a rational judgement as to whether the act was right or wrong, but also the ability to exercise will power to control physical acts, in accordance with rational judgement."

It is also important to note that while for hospital order cases the psychiatrist gives his opinion as to the offender's state of mind when he is examined, for the purposes of a diminished responsibility defence, the psychiatrist has to try to discover the offender's state of mind, not when he is examined, but at the time when the offence was committed.

It is quite possible that the act involved in the offence itself can relieve the offender's feelings to some extent and help him to recover so that by the time he is examined by a psychiatrist he no longer suffers from depression or ceases to be suicidal.[21]

Another point worth noting is that while the transient effect of alcohol is not a mental abnormality,[22] if a slight abnormality already exists and is aggravated by alcohol, then psychiatrists do usually give the opinion that the offender's mental responsibility was substantially impaired.[23] Also where alcoholism had reached such a level as to injure the brain or where the drinking had become involuntary, the defence could still be available; but not if the defendant simply did not resist an impulse to drink.[24]

Under section 2(1) of the Homicide Act 1957 the diminished responsibility defence is available only when the offender suffers from arrested or retarded development, or his abnormality is inherent or brought about by disease or injury.

## 8. Reduction in hospital orders

A recent study of the diminished responsibility defence[25] showed that there had been a large reduction in the proportion of diminished responsibility cases which received hospital orders. This was undoubtedly due to the fact that psychiatrists had recommended far fewer cases for hospital orders, which meant that judges were deprived of the opportunity to make such orders and instead of making more use of non-custodial sentences, they made up the shortfall in hospital orders by a proportionate increase in prison sentences.

One can understand, although not necessarily agree with, the need to send a psychopathic killer to prison, if no hospital order can be made to a secure hospital; but it is difficult to understand this in cases where there is no risk of further homicide: if, for instance, a compassionate spouse kills to relieve suffering, as in *R. v. Morris.*[26] A prison sentence in such circumstances cannot even act as a deterrent. One is forced to the view that such prison sentences can only be justified on grounds of retribution. This runs counter to the common law principle of not convicting someone who was so mentally disordered at the time of the offence that it would be unreasonable to attribute guilt to him.

## 9. Proposal for reviewable prison sentences

It would be fairer to diminished responsibility cases which end in life sentences, if the Butler Committee's recommendation for a reviewable prison sentence was implemented.[28] This would mean that there would not be such a vast difference between the release of life prisoners, usually about 9 years, and release from Special Hospitals, usually about 4 years or less, where virtually the same considerations apply to both groups.[29] If this recommendation were to be implemented there would be an annual review of life prisoners, whose responsibility was diminished, in the same way as there is for restricted patients under section 41(6) of the Mental Health Act 1983. The only criterion for release for reviewable prison sentences would be public safety without any punitive elements being taken into account.

## 10. Conclusion

The diminished responsibility defence is still necessary in view of the mandatory life sentence for murder, even though it is no longer a capital offence. In murder cases, no mitigating circumstances can be taken into account even though all murders are not of the same seriousness in many respects. Judges should not be forced to pass the same sentence in a mercy killing case as in a planned killing for gain. Those who argue for retaining a mandatory sentence for murder usually base their argument on the ground that murder is a unique offence and needs a unique deterrent. However, a life sentence is not as effective a deterrent as all that. It is accepted by everyone that a life sentence does not mean imprisonment for life.

Another reason often given by those who advocate the retention of the mandatory sentence for murder, is that judges can not predict when it would be safe to release the defendant. Yet they already do so in diminished responsibility cases, which are far more difficult.[30] There seems no reason therefore why they should not be able to sentence in the same way mentally normal murderers.

If life imprisonment became a maximum rather than a mandatory sentence for murder, then the diminished responsibility defence would probably become irrelevant and could be abolished. However, there would be no harm in the defence continuing until it is seen to have fallen into disuse. It serves a most useful purpose in introducing some flexibility and justice into the sentencing for offences which would otherwise be murder.

## CHAPTER 4: AMERICAN COMPARISON

### 1. Brief background

In America the main defence for those suffering from mental abnormality is that of insanity, which is variously described as such, or as mental disorder or non-responsibility. Some courts and legislatures in America additionally recognise that someone suffering from mental abnormality can not have the required "mens rea," which they call the "diminished capacity" doctrine. There is a third possibility in some states of America: a verdict of "guilty but mentally ill." Unlike the insanity defence, the latter defences of diminished capacity and guilty but mentally ill do not usually lead to acquittal but are taken into consideration in sentencing.

In the nineteenth century and even before, American courts applied the principles of the English McNaghten Rules, which have frequently been embodied in statutes.[1] However, in some states there are variations to the McNaghten Rules. The New York statute, for example, provides that the defence of insanity involves the loss of the ability to distinguish right from wrong in regard to the act or to know the nature or quality of that act due to mental impairment. It defines "know" very broadly. It requires only that the accused lacked "substantial capacity to know or appreciate" the nature and "consequences" of the conduct or its "wrongfulness".[2] Some statutes obscure the issue by avoiding the use of "know" or equivalent words.[3]

The Georgia statute, for example, poses the question whether the accused had "the mental capacity to distinguish between right and wrong."[4] In spite of this one is still thrown back on deciding whether "distinguishing" between right and wrong involves the minimal intellectual awareness.

Before the McNaghten Rules of 1843 American case law had developed some basis for making the defence available where the defendant's impairment had not affected his cognitive abilities but had prevented him from exercising normal control over his behaviour. What some American writers refer to as "volitional impairment."[5] This later became the "irresistible impulse" criterion, which meant that the defendant was entitled to acquittal upon a finding that a mental disorder had caused him to experience an irresistible and uncontrollable impulse to commit the offence, even if he remained able to understand the nature of the offence and its wrongfulness.

The impairment required for the irresistible impulse defence had to be sudden. Thus it did not accommodate impairments that destroyed volition but developed slowly and perhaps insidiously.[6] The states, which adopted the irresistible impulse defence, added it to the McNaghten Rules so that a defendant became entitled to acquittal upon showing that he either came within the McNaghten Rules or the irresistible impulse test.[7]

## 2. Model penal code

The American Law Institute's Model Penal Code promulgated in 1962 proposed a defence along the lines that the defendant was entitled to be acquitted, if as a result of mental disease or defect, he either lacked "substantial capacity to appreciate the criminality of his conduct or to conform his conduct to the requirements of law." This proposal was widely adopted, although some States slightly modified it. For example Missouri substituted for "substantial impairment" the test whether the defendant was "incapable of conforming his conduct to the requirements of law," or, in the case of cognitive impairment, that the defendant "did not know or appreciate" the wrongfulness of his conduct.[8] The courts in America also adopted the Model Penal Code's proposal. For example, it was adopted in *People v. Drew*[9] by the Californian Supreme Court which up to then had applied only the McNaghten Rules.

The court's reasoning in *People v. Drew* was that "current psychiatric opinion ... holds that mental illness often leaves the individual's intellectual understanding relatively unimpaired, but so affects his emotions or reason that he is unable to prevent himself from committing the act." Alabama Supreme Court in *Parsons v. State*[10] in defining the volitional impairment test said:

> "It is no satisfactory objection to say that the rule permitting reliance upon volitional impairment is of difficult application. The rule in McNaghten's Case... is equally obnoxious to a like criticism... We think we can safely rely in this matter upon the intelligence of our juries, guided by the testimony of men who have practically made a study of the disease of insanity."

Some American case law tends to define insanity in a very negative way. For example, in *Korsak v. State*[11] it was said:

> "[Whatever mental condition did exist,] it must exist because of disease of the mind... mere immorality or lasciviousness impelling one to commit an act not due to a disease of the mind, would not be a defence."

This is very similar to the proviso to the definitions of "mental disorder," ''severe mental impairment," "mental impairment" and "psychopathic disorder" in section 1(2) and (3) of the Mental Health Act 1983 in England and Wales, where "promiscuity or other immoral conduct, sexual deviancy or dependence on alcohol or drugs'' are expressly excluded from the definitions.

### 3. Constitutional constraints

There are also cases which show that where states have attempted to preclude a defence of insanity, on the grounds that it was abused, they were held to be in breach of the constitution. For instance, in *State v. Strasberg*[12] the Washington Supreme Court expressed the view that legislation abolishing the insanity defence would violate the state's constitutional requirement of due process. In *Powell v. Texas*[13] the defendant, who was a chronic alcoholic, agreed that once he took a drink he lost control over all his subsequent action. He argued that to punish him, therefore, for what amounted to involuntary acts violated the Eighth Amendment to the Federal Constitution, which prohibited cruel and unusual punishment. The Supreme Court delivered a majority judgement (5:4) that the Eighth Amendment prohibited criminal conviction for conduct which resulted from an "irresistible urge."

### 4. Diminished capacity

By the early twentieth century, some American courts had accepted the argument that a defendant's mental abnormality could, apart from its significance on the insanity issue, also, or alternatively, form the basis of a challenge to the adequacy of proof of "mens rea." This particularly applied to first degree premeditated murder, where the defence could challenge the prosecution's proof of the required premeditation due to the defendant's mental incapacity. This became known as the defence of "diminished capacity."[14] The defence applied also, of course, to any other offence of specific intent.

The defence of diminished capacity did not result in acquittal, as the insanity defence did; but, as acknowledged by the California

Supreme Court in *People v. Henderson*,[15] simply reduced the seriousness of the offence. Not unlike, in this respect, the British diminished responsibility defence under section 2(2) of the Homicide Act 1957, which reduces murder to manslaughter.

In fact in California the defence of diminished capacity was limited to homicide and the definitions of homicide were changed to introduce a clearer "mens rea" element, which the defence could rebut. Thus in *People v. Wolff*[16] the California Supreme Court held that first degree premeditated murder required that the defendant "maturely and meaningfully reflect upon the gravity of "the contemplated killing and that this be done with adequate realisation "of the enormity" of the nature of the act. If the defendant's mental impairment caused his reflection or realisation to materially fall below this requirement, he could not be guilty of first degree murder.

*People v. Poddar*[17] went even further and held that the malice aforethought necessary for proving second degree murder also required that the defendant be able to act within the law. If, because of his impairment, he was unable to act within the laws regulating society, he would be guilty of only manslaughter. Thus the court sought to grade defendants' liability for homicide by reference in part to any mental impairment, including volitional impairment they may have had at the time of the killing.[18]

However, these efforts of the California Supreme Court to grade the defendant's liability for homicide from acquittal, if he pleaded insanity, to a finding of manslaughter, if he pleaded that his mental abnormality rendered him unaware of his duty to act within the law, to second degree murder, if his mental abnormality caused him not to reflect adequately upon the significance of a contemplated killing. was rejected by the state legislature.

Section 189 of the California Penal Code 1981 provided that to prove that a first degree murder was "deliberate and premeditated it shall not be necessary to prove that the defendant maturely and meaningfully reflected upon the gravity of his or her act."

In defining second degree murder, section 188 of the California Penal Code 1981 provided that "an awareness of the obligation to act within the general body of laws regulating society is not included within the definition of malice." The following year this provision was amended to provide that "acting despite such awareness" is similarly not included within the definition of malice.

Section 21[b] of the California Penal Code 1982 further provided that "evidence that the accused lacked capacity or ability to control his conduct for any reason shall not be admissible on the issue of whether the accused actually had any mental state with respect to the commission of any crime."

Thus the California Penal Code 1982 after declaring that "as a matter of public policy there shall be no defence of diminished capacity, diminished responsibility or irresistible impulse in a criminal action" went on to provide positively that "evidence of mental disease, mental defect, or mental disorder shall not be admitted to negate the capacity to form any mental state, including, but not limited to, purpose, intent, knowledge or malice aforethought, with which the accused committed the act. Evidence of mental disease, mental defect or mental disorder is admissible on the issue as to whether the criminal defendant actually formed any such mental state."[19]

These provisions of the California Penal Code show how difficult it is to try to grade liability according to the defendant's psychological impairments. This difficulty is of course increased if one tries to integrate volitional impairment into the grading process.[20]

However, unless adequate provisions are made in the state legislatures for mentally disordered defendants, constitutional problems arise. For example, in *Hendershott v. People*[21] it was held that a Colorado provision limiting the use of evidence of impaired mental conditions to "specific intent" offences was unconstitutional as violating the defendant's right to due process of law.

Some authors on American law[22] have urged that mental impairment should be relevant only if it shows the absence of "mens rea" required by the crime charged. Montana was the only American state which had adopted this "mens rea" approach as the sole defence for mentally disordered offenders.[23] This was hardly satisfactory as it would exclude from the defence mental disorder induced delusions or hallucinations.

In most states someone who believes in a state of facts, which if true would excuse the offence, would be acquitted. For example, the defendant would be acquitted if the mental disorder induced a mistaken belief that some one is about to kill the defendant and he killed that person in self-defence. However, under the "mens rea" approach, such a defendant would not be acquitted.[24]

There could of course be similar acquittals under English law. Hale,[25] for instance, gives the example of a soldier on sentry duty at night, who shot and killed one of his own officers, whom he reasonably thought to be one of the enemy, being acquitted of murder. Another unsatisfactory aspect of the Montana legislation was that the defence was not available to anyone charged with a "non specific intent" offence.

## 5. Diminished responsibility

Until recently there was no "diminished responsibility" defence generally available in America. Some American writers had suggested that this should be introduced, at any rate, at the sentencing stage.[26] Nor do most American jurisdictions have non-penal commitments to treatment although a court probably can make the receipt of treatment a condition of probation.

There is a federal constitutional requirement that there should not be a mandatory death penalty on the ground that this would violate the Eighth Amendment to the United States Constitution, which prohibits cruel and unusual punishment.[27] It is reasonably clear from cases like *Gregg v. Georgia*[28] that in murder cases the sentencing court must have discretion in choosing a death sentence or imprisonment and this discretion should be exercised on criteria laid down in legislation.

This is clearly much more satisfactory than the mandatory sentence for murder in England. Most states in America comply with this requirement by making provision in their relevant statutes by listing all of the potentially aggravating and mitigating considerations. Then they provide that following conviction for a capital offence, a sentencing hearing is to be held to decide whether any aggravating or mitigating factors exist. At such hearing both the prosecution and defence are entitled to produce evidence.

Although there are no Supreme Court decisions on the point, obviously mental impairment must be one of the mitigating factors to be specified in the legislation.[29] For example, in the Florida Laws 1972, one of the mitigating circumstances to be considered is whether "the capacity of the defendant to appreciate the criminality of his conduct, or to conform his conduct to the requirements of law, was substantially impaired."

Another recent development in America is the verdict of "guilty but mentally ill," which is usually taken to be based on the 1975 Michigan legislation. The aim of this legislation was to reduce the number of what were perceived to be improper insanity acquittals, without creating further problems by totally abolishing the insanity defence.[30] The jury has to be instructed that they can find the defendant guilty but mentally ill if it is proved beyond all reasonable doubt that the defendant is guilty of the offence charged and that he was mentally ill but not legally insane at the time of the commission of the offence.

Mental illness in this context is defined as substantial disorder of thought or mood which significantly impairs judgement, behaviour, capacity to recognise reality or ability to cope with ordinary demands of life."

When a defendant is found to be "guilty but mentally ill" the court has the option of committing him to the Department of Corrections where "he shall undergo further evaluation and be given such treatment as is psychiatricaly indicated for his mental illness or retardation." Should he be paroled, the completion of any treatment which was commenced during his incarceration has to be made a condition of parole. Failure to continue treatment is a basis for parole revocation.[31]

However, it was found that the Michigan scheme had not in fact reduced acquittals on insanity grounds.[32] It was also found that defendants found to be guilty but mentally ill were not likely to receive any more or better mental health care than defendants convicted and simply sentenced.[33]

The Indiana Supreme Court upheld that state's guilty but mentally ill provisions, which are similar to those of Michigan, against a number of constitutional attacks. Including an argument in *Taylor v. State*[34] that the definitions were so vague as to create an unacceptable risk of arbitrary application.

On the other hand, Criss and Raine[35] found that the "mentally ill" defence was working satisfactorily. The percentage of those acquitted on the ground of insanity and found to have no serious mental disorder had decreased from 43.8 per cent in 1974 to 12.1 per cent in 1979.

## 6. Burden of proof

In some states it is for the prosecution to prove that the defendant was responsible for his actions. Indeed, in *Davis v. United States*[36] the United States Supreme Court held that the burden of proving responsibility was on the prosecution. As a result a defendant was entitled to be acquitted if the trier of fact entertained a reasonable doubt as to whether or not he was responsible. But in *Leland v. Oregon*[37] the Court held that a state rule requiring a defendant to prove insanity by proof beyond a reasonable doubt did not deny a state defendant his federal constitutional right to due process of law.

In *Re Winship*[38] it was decided that the due process clause of the Fourteenth Amendment protects the accused in state criminal proceedings against conviction "except upon proof beyond a reasonable doubt of every fact necessary to constitute proof of the crime with which he is charged." This would seem to impose a limit on the extent to which state legislatures can shift to the defendant the burden of proof; but the extent of this limit is unclear.[39]

## 7. Sentencing of insane offenders

Originally America followed the English common law rule that those found to be insane were entitled to unconditional acquittal. When the English Criminal Lunatics Act 1800 provided for the detention of such offenders during His Majesty's pleasure, American jurisdictions adopted similar procedures.[40] In *Jackson v. Indiana*[41] the court found that federal constitutional doctrines prohibited the subjection of mentally disordered defendants to commitment under a more lenient commitment standard and a more stringent release standard than were applicable to mentally disordered persons committed on a "civil" basis.

Usually civil commitment can not take place unless it can be shown that the proposed patient poses a substantial threat of serious physical harm to himself or others. Such commitments are not open ended but limited in duration until such time as the patient recovers.[42]

Usually juries are not told what sentences may be imposed if they find the defendant guilty. This is left to the judge.[43] Thus the jury are left to determine the sufficiency of the evidence to prove a defendant's guilt without reference to the consequences which may follow.

The traditional position in America, followed by a majority of states,[44] is that the insanity defence does not justify an exception to this general rule. On the other hand, quite a substantial minority of states, recognise an exception to the general rule and provide that the jury should be directed as to the basic procedural consequences of a verdict of not guilty by reason of insanity. The District of Columbia Circuit Court of Appeals required such directions on the sentence which follows conviction in *Taylor v. United States*[45] and reaffirmed this requirement in *Lyles v. United States*.[46] Other states have followed the "Lyles Rule" in cases like *People v. Thompson*[47] and *State v. Nuckolls*.[48]

The reason given in *Lyles v. United States* for the insistence on these directions on sentence was that, in the absence of such directions, jurors would probably assume that acquittal would result in outright release. Such an assumption would distort the jurors' evaluation of the evidence relating to insanity, given their likely desire to avoid having a dangerous and mentally disordered person turned loose in the community.

The objections to the "Lyles Rule" are that evaluation of the evidence on insanity should be made without regard to the consequences and secondly such directions can never be complete. As decided in *Curry v. State*[49] no directions to the jury can "give a jury complete and accurate information about all the possible future decisions with respect to a person found to be not guilty by reason of insanity."

## 8. The Durham formula

The District of Columbia applied the Durham formula for about 20 years. *Durham v. United States*[50] laid down the principle that "an accused is not criminally responsible if his unlawful act was the product of mental disease or defect." In that case Judge Bazelon attempted to extend the psychiatrists' role in such cases by allowing them to provide all possible relevant information concerning all aspects of the accused's psychiatric diagnosis. Thus even a very remote mental disturbance could be argued to have resulted in the accused's unlawful act. The judge's reason for such a liberal formula was that "our collective conscience does not allow punishment where it can not impose blame."

However, this meant that psychiatrists by giving their opinion on whether the mental abnormality had resulted in the unlawful act were usurping the functions of the jury. In *Browner v. United States*[51] Judge Bazelon himself complained that psychiatrists had a "stranglehold" on the jury's opinions. The Durham formula has now fallen into virtual disuse.

While the Butler Report[52] states that the drawback of the Durham formula is that it encouraged psychiatrists to draw inferences which are not for doctors to draw, it fails in its own proposals, for the replacement of the McNaghten Rules, to provide that the accused's unlawful act should have a causal link with the accused's mental disorder.[53] However, by providing a strict definition of severe mental illness, the Butler Report ensures that under its proposal, the psychiatrists would give evidence on the factual tests, the determination of which would be left to the jury. Thus the psychiatrists would not testify to "the naked conclusion."

## 9. The Hinckley case[54]

On March 1981 John Hinckley fired gunshots which wounded the then President Ronald Reagan and three other persons outside the

Hilton Hotel in Washington DC. His motive was a desire to develop a personal relationship with the actress Jodie Foster. Hinckley pleaded insanity. The jury were told that the Government had the obligation to prove sanity beyond a reasonable doubt. Unlike the position in England, where it is for the defence to prove insanity on a balance of probabilities. The jury were told under the "Lyles Rule," what the consequences of a finding of not guilty by reason of insanity would be.

There was public outcry when a verdict of not guilty by reason of insanity was returned. The public, while acknowledging that the trial judge and jury had simply applied the existing law, thought that the result was in some way improper and demanded a revision of the law relating to the defence of insanity.[55]

However, little if anything, was done by way of reform.[56] The limiting of the insanity defence to simply rebutting "mens rea" was again considered but almost unanimously rejected. Several states made provision for an alternative verdict of "guilty but mentally ill."[57] The Delaware Laws 1982,[58] for instance, provide that a "guilty but insane" verdict should be returned if it is determined "that, at the time of the conduct charged, a defendant suffered from a psychiatric disorder which substantially disturbed such person's thinking, feeling or behaviour and/or that such psychiatric disorder left such person with insufficient willpower to choose whether he would do the act or refrain from doing it, although physically capable."

The National Mental Health Association issued a report in March 1983 (National Commission on Insanity Defence 1983). This report recommended that, instead of a verdict of "not guilty by reason of insanity," there should be substituted a verdict of "not responsible by reason of insanity." This was not a new suggestion as the Indiana Laws of 1978 already made provision for such a verdict.[59]

The Reagan Administration's Comprehensive Crime Control Act 1983 proposed, as a federal statutory responsibility standard, a cognitive criterion; thus abandoning the impairment of volition defence. Several states have already repealed the "volition prong" of the insanity standard based on the Model Penal Code.[60]

Another result of the *Hinckley Case* was the shift of the burden of proving insanity from the prosecution to the defence. Most states have imposed on the defendant "a preponderance of evidence" level of proof, much the same as in England.[61] Some states, however, have imposed a higher level of proof on the defendant, following the Reagan Administration's proposals of 1983, by requiring "clear and convincing evidence."[62]

In *Jones v. United States*[63] the Supreme Court challenged some of the aspects of the *Hinckley Case* by holding that "when a criminal defendant established, by a preponderance of the evidence, that he is not guilty of a crime by reason of insanity, the Constitution permits the Government, on the basis of the insanity judgement, to confine him to a mental institution until such time as he has regained his sanity or is no longer a danger to himself or society." This is very similar to the grounds for release by a Mental Health Review Tribunal in England under section 72(1) of the Mental Health Act 1983.

Thus a brief review of the American system of dealing with mentally disordered offenders is useful in showing some of the dead-ends they have reached, such as limiting the insanity defence to negating "mens rea." Both the English and the American systems having started off from the same common law principles and the McNaghten Rules, it seems that there are useful lessons which each country could learn from the other. These are examined below.

## 10. Possible developments in light of American cases

Following the Hinckley acquittal and the Jones case, two trends seem likely to develop in America. One is that discharge following acquittal on grounds of insanity will probably become a judicial matter. The other is that acquitting courts will probably be given jurisdiction to consider the question of discharge.[64]

Before these developments can take place, the point, which will have to be resolved, is whether it will be constitutionally acceptable, in jurisdictions in which civilly committed persons may be discharged at the discretion of the treating authorities, for discharge to be at the discretion of the court instead. In England, for instance, following the decision of the European Court of Human Rights in *X. v. United Kingdom*, the Mental Health Act 1983 has put restricted offenders on the same footing regarding release, as civil patients. Thus in this respect America could well benefit from the English system of Mental Health Review Tribunals.

In turn, English law could usefully adopt some of the American concepts, such as a much more co-ordinated role for central Government, if not a new Department along the lines of the American Department of Correction, so that once a court has decided to make a hospital order then it would become a duty on the central Government to provide the necessary treatment.

As has already been pointed out by some writers[64] while there is a duty on the Home Office to provide adequate prison accommodation once a court has decided to send an offender to prison, there is not a similar duty on the Department of Health to provide hospital accommodation once a court has decided to make a hospital order. Except of course in the case of the special verdict under section 5 of the Criminal Procedure (Insanity) Act 1964, as substituted by the Criminal Procedure (Insanity and Unfitness to Plead) Act 1991.

While the Butler Report has made many helpful suggestions for reform, it is a shortcoming in that Report that it did not suggest a duty to provide the necessary hospital accommodation, whenever a court is minded to make a hospital order under section 37 of the Mental Health Act 1983 or following a verdict of manslaughter due to diminished responsibility. On the contrary, it suggested giving more discretion to psychiatrists and hospital managers at the expense of cutting down the discretion of the courts in making hospital orders.[65] It is, however, only fair to point out that at the time of the Butler Report, the problem regarding the shortage of hospital accommodation was not as acute as it is today, indeed if it was a problem at all in the mid-1970s.

In America the impetus for reform has come from the public outrage following Hinckley's acquittal on grounds of insanity. Although there would appear to be no justification for it,[66] the public were convinced that the insanity defence was being pleaded in too many cases where there was no justification for it. In England by contrast, the insanity defence has virtually fallen into disuse and is hardly ever pleaded and its revival is being considered in a far more calm atmosphere since the Butler Committee Report proposals and the proposal for the codification of the Criminal law by the Law Commission.[67]

While the discussion on possible reforms continues, it is possible to draw conclusions from the American attempts at reform following the *Hinckley Case*. The attempted reforms in America vary from those who wish to abolish a separate defence of insanity to those who wish to introduce a modified form of the McNaghten Rules. The common thread running through all the suggested reforms is the perceived need to restrict the use of the defence.

None of the reforms, which have so far been introduced in America are fully satisfactory and would not serve as models for reform of the insanity defence in England. However, they are worth examining to see if any lessons can be learnt, even if the lesson is simply not to go down a particular road as it has been tried and does not lead anywhere.

One approach, already followed in Montana, Idaho and Utah, is to abolish the insanity defence and rely on the "mens rea " element of an offence for the acquittal of those who could not have formed the necessary intent due to their mental disorder. However, this is too narrow because it would be limited to "those cases where the defendant at the time of the offence was so seriously mentally ill that he did not have the required intent or state of mind required to commit an illegal act."[68] It would exclude from the scope of the defence those who had the requisite intent but were acting under a delusion induced by their mental illness.

In this sense therefore, the Montana approach would not be an improvement on the McNaghten Rules but a retrogressive step. Nor would this solution be as satisfactory as the Butler proposals as it deals only with the first limb of those proposals. However widely the courts interpret "mens rea" those who were severely mentally ill and who killed under a delusion, for example that God had told them to rid the world of prostitutes, would still be found guilty, in spite of severe mental illness.

Another approach of keeping the insanity defence but providing an alternative verdict of "guilty but mentally ill" raises the difficulty of deciding when the verdict of guilty but mentally ill would be appropriate rather than a verdict of insanity. This approach has been followed in several states, including Michigan, Alaska, Georgia, Pennsylvania and Kentucky. Under the Michigan Law[69] a defendant can be found guilty but mentally ill if it is proved beyond a reasonable doubt that he committed the offence and he was mentally ill at the time but not legally insane.

In this latter approach the definitions of mentally ill and insanity overlap and in Pennsylvania they are exactly the same.[70] This means that psychiatrists and juries are given no criteria in deciding which verdict is more appropriate in any particular case. Thus either verdict can be returned. This approach achieves little while giving the impression that action has been taken in response to the public unease about the verdict in the *Hinckley Case*.

A third approach to reform has been to revert to a modified form of the McNaghten Rules. Thus the Federal Law, under which Hinckley was tried, has been changed by the Insanity Defence Reform Act 1984. That Act makes provision for the defence of insanity where the defendant "as a result of a severe mental disease or defect was unable to appreciate the nature and quality or the wrongfulness of his acts."[71] Although the courts have done their best to interpret this variation of the McNaghten Rules as widely as possible, it is still not wide enough and could lead to a virtual elimination of the insanity defence, as admitted by the Supreme Court of California in *People v. Skinner*[72] and as indeed has happened in England.

Clause 38 of the Draft Criminal Code in England[73] substitutes for the McNaghten Rules a verdict of "not guilty by reason of mental disorder," as proposed in Chapter 18 of the Butler Report. It provides that such a verdict should be returned either, under clause 38(l)(a), when the defendant committed the offence charged but was at the time suffering from severe mental disorder; or under clause 38(l)(b), when the evidence of the defendant's mental disorder at the time of his act is the reason why he is not proved to have committed the act charged. In each case, the mental disorder has to be proved on the balance of probabilities by either the prosecution or the defendant.

Clause 38(2) of the Draft Criminal Code defines "mental disorder" along the lines of the definition in section 1(2) of the Mental Health Act 1983. Thus, unlike the present position in respect of the making of hospital orders under section 37(2)(a) of the 1983 Act, "any other disorder or disability of mind" is included in the definition. The definition of "severe mental illness" in clause 38(2)(e) of the Code is put in square brackets because, as paragraph 12.7 of the Law Commission Report states, it is certain to receive close professional scrutiny and may well call for amendment before it is enacted.

Clause 41 of the Code relegates the disposal to be made after a mental disorder verdict to Schedule 4, but paragraph 12.29 of the Law Commission Report proposes that the court should have flexible disposal powers. This flexibility follows the Butler proposal[74] and is now reflected in the Criminal Procedure (Insanity and Unfitness to Plead) Act 1991.

Although nothing has yet been done about the rest of the suggested reforms of the insanity defence, the Law Commission's work in this field has been valuable in focusing attention once more on the inadequacy of the English insanity defence, just as the *Hinckley Case* did in America.

CHAPTER 5: ANALYSIS OF THE 1982 AMENDMENTS

## 1. New definitions

Some of the amendments made by the Mental Health (Amendment) Act 1982 were in response to the decision of the European Court of Human Rights in *X. v. United Kingdom*;[1] others implemented some of the proposals of the Butler Committee;[2] and some are improvements introduced by the Government as a result of their own Consultation Document[3] published in 1976. A White Paper[4] was published in 1978 and a White Paper[5] was also published in 1981 with the Mental Health (Amendment) Bill. However, the principal concern of the 1982 Act was to improve the safeguards available to detained patients.

Apart from changes, such as substituting for "subnormality" and "severe subnormality," "mental impairment" and "severe mental impairment," the 1982 Act introduced into those definitions the concept of "abnormally aggressive or seriously irresponsible conduct." It also added to the exceptions from the definitions of mental disorder "sexual deviancy or dependence on alcohol or drugs" as well as repeating the words "promiscuity or other immoral conduct," which were in section 4(5) of the 1959 Act.

Under the Mental Health Act 1959 the differences between "severe subnormality" and "subnormality" were more marked. For "severe subnormality" the arrested or incomplete development of mind had to be such as to make the patient "incapable of living an independent life or of guarding himself against serious exploitation." For "subnormality" the arrested or incomplete development of mind had to be such as to require or be susceptible "to medical treatment or other special care or training of the patient." Not forgetting that "medical treatment" in this context is defined (now in section 145(1) of the 1983 Act) as including nursing and "care, habilitation and rehabilitation under medical supervision."

Both the concept of treatability and being able to guard against serious exploitation, although left out of the definitions, can be found elsewhere in the Amending Act of 1982 and consequently in the 1983 consolidation. Treatability is in section 19(4) of the 1982 Act (now section 37(2)(a)(i) of the 1983 Act) and section 39(3) of the 1982 Act (now 72(2)(a) of the 1983 Act). In the case of the minor disorders of psychopathic disorder or mental impairment, before making a hospital order (now under section 37 of the 1983 Act) the court must be satisfied "that such treatment is likely to alleviate or prevent a deterioration of his condition." Also under section 39(3) of the 1982 Act before directing the discharge of certain patients, a Mental Health Review Tribunal must have regard to the treatability test, which here applies to the major disorders of mental illness and severe mental impairment as well. (See now section 72(2)(a) of the 1983 Act).

The concept of leading an independent life and guarding against serious exploitation is in section 39(3) of the 1982 Act (now section 72(2)(b) of the 1983 Act). That is to say, in determining whether to direct the discharge of certain patients, a Mental Health Review Tribunal must have regard to, in the case of the major disorders alone, the likelihood of the patient, if discharged, "being able to care for himself against serious exploitation."

The distinction between "severe mental impairment" and "mental impairment" is now simply one of degree. (See section 1(2) of the 1982 Act and section 1(2) of the 1983 Act). In the case of "severe mental impairment" the impairment of intelligence and social functioning has to be "severe," while in the case of "mental impairment" the impairment of intelligence and social functioning has to be "significant." The legal difference between "severe" and "significant" is not clear. Obviously "mental impairment" is less severe but this does not take the definition much further and leaves it completely in the hands of psychiatrists to decide which it is with no guidance whatsoever. Different legal consequences follow from a diagnosis of "mental impairment" as opposed to "severe mental impairment." In the latter case, there is no treatability test. This can make all the difference between a hospital order and long term of imprisonment.

The change in the definition section from "subnormality" to "mental impairment" means that a great majority of the mentally handicapped now fall outside section 37 and more significantly the civil commitment powers of the 1983 Act, unless their condition is associated with abnormally aggressive or seriously irresponsible conduct.

## 2. More frequent access to tribunals

In general, the amendments introduced by the 1982 Act mean shorter periods of detention and more frequent access to the Mental Health Review Tribunals. The periods at the expiration of which most patients can apply to a tribunal were reduced from 12 months to 6 months. So far as mentally disordered offenders are concerned, restriction directions imposed on those transferred from prison now expire at the earliest date of release with remission. This was a proposal made by MIND.[6]

The 1982 Act also makes provision for remands to hospital for a medical report or for treatment and for interim hospital orders; all of which were proposed by the Butler Committee.[7] The object of an interim hospital order being to enable an alleged offender to be examined and treated in hospital for a limited period (up to 6 months) before a final decision is taken. Presumably if the interim hospital order is not a success then the court could pass a prison sentence on the offender when he is returned to court. This would of course be most unjust.[8] It would be preferable, where the court is not sure whether a hospital order is the most suitable way of disposing of the case, to use the remand powers to hospital for report or for treatment.

Under section 30 of the 1982 Act (now section 36 of the 1983 Act) remands to hospital for treatment can be made only by the Crown Court and for the major disorders. Two medical recommendations are needed. The remand is only for 28 days but can be extended so as not to exceed 12 weeks in all.

Under section 29 of the 1982 Act (now section 35 of the 1983 Act) the period for remands to hospital for report on the offender's mental condition is the same, but they can be made for all four categories of mental disorder and are not restricted to the Crown Court. Only one medical recommendation is necessary. According to the Earl of Dundee (Lords Hansard 7th November 1988, col. 524) in 1986 only 304 remands were made under section 35 of the 1983 Act which compares with 7,055 reports prepared by prison medical officers on people remanded to prison for psychiatric assessment.

## 3. Extension of powers of Mental Health Review Tribunals

The 1982 Act also implemented the decision of the European Court of Human Rights in *X. v. United Kingdom*.[9] Under Article 5(1) of the European Convention on Human Rights no one can be deprived of his liberty save in specified cases in accordance with law. Of the exhaustive list of exceptions in Article 5(1), the relevant sub-paragraph for a mentally disordered person is sub-paragraph (e), which provides for the detention of persons of unsound mind. That sub-paragraph states that the detention must be "in accordance with a procedure prescribed by law" and it must be a "lawful detention." The first limb implies that the procedure must not be arbitrary. The second limb implies, as decided in paragraph 39 of the *Winterwerp* judgement,[10] that except in cases of emergency, the individual must be shown to be of unsound mind on the basis of objective medical evidence; the mental disorder must be of a kind or degree justifying compulsory detention and the validity of the continued detention must depend on the persistence of the mental disorder.

Section 66 of the Mental Health Act 1959 (now section 42 of the 1983 Act) gave the Home Secretary a very wide discretion in discharging a restricted patient, either absolutely or subject to conditions, "as he thinks fit." Further, the Secretary of State could "at any time" recall to hospital a restricted patient who had been discharged conditionally. The court held that unless the Home Secretary, on medical evidence before him, decided that the person to be recalled came within the definition of "patient" in section 147(1) of the Mental Health Act 1959 (now section 145(1) of the 1983 Act) no power of recall should arise.

Even where the mental patient has been convicted by a competent court and therefore comes within the exception in subparagraph (a) of Article 5(1) of the Convention, the provisions of Article 5(4) would probably still be breached as there would be no limitation on the period of detention.

The Mental Health (Amendment) Act 1982 overcomes the criticism in *X. v. United Kingdom* by making provision, in section 28 and Schedules 1 and 3 (now sections 40 and 41 and Schedule 1 of the 1983 Act), for offenders detained under restriction orders to apply for discharge once every twelve months to a Mental Health Review Tribunal and for those Tribunals to be able to order their discharge. The Home Secretary's discretion for ordering the discharge of mental patients is preserved in section 42 of the Mental Health Act 1983. In spite of this, however, Mental Health Review Tribunals, chaired in these cases by a circuit judge or recorder, now play a far greater part in the discharge of patients subject to restrictions without a time limit.

## 4. Transfer directions

Section 22 of the 1982 Act amended section 72 of the 1959 Act (now section 47 of the 1983 Act) so that the Home Secretary, when transferring a person serving a prison sentence to hospital, has to be satisfied that the nature or degree of the mental disorder is such as to make it "appropriate" for the prisoner to be detained in hospital rather than "warranting" his detention in hospital.

As before, the Home Secretary still has to be satisfied, on the reports of two doctors (one approved under section 12 of the 1983

Act), that the prisoner is suffering from mental illness, severe mental impairment, mental impairment or psychopathic disorder. The Home Secretary also still has to consider, having regard to the public interest and all the circumstances of the case, that it is expedient to make a transfer direction. Such direction can be made with or without restrictions on discharge. Usually restrictions are imposed unless the transfer is made a month or less before the earliest date of release.[11]

If a restricted offender is cured or no further treatment can be given for his disorder, the Home Secretary can either discharge him, if he would have been eligible for release on parole or return him to prison to serve the rest of his sentence. Under section 24 of the 1982 Act (now section 50 of the 1983 Act) a restriction direction ceases on the date when his prison sentence comes to an end, taking into account any remission he would have been given.

In the case of those who have been committed for trial under section 25 of the 1982 Act (now section 51 of the 1983 Act) the transfer direction ceases to have effect when the case is finally disposed of by the court or if he is cured or no further treatment can be given for his disorder. The Home Secretary can then remit him back to a place where he might have been detained if no transfer direction had been made. Otherwise the court can remit him into custody or release him on bail, in which case the direction ceases to have effect.

Section 28(3) of the 1982 Act increased the monitoring of restricted patients by requiring the Responsible Medical Officer to furnish an annual report to the Home Secretary (now sections 41(6) and 49(3) of the 1983 Act).

The provisions of section 28 and Schedule 1 of the 1982 Act give extended powers to Mental Health Review Tribunals in relation to restricted patients. Paragraph 8(1)(a) of Schedule 1 to the 1982 Act enables Rules of Procedure to restrict the persons who can sit as President of a Tribunal. Thus the Mental Health Review Tribunal Rules 1983 (S.I. No. 842), made under section 78 of the 1983 Act, provide in rule 8(3) that only those legal members, who have been approved by the Lord Chancellor for the purpose of considering applications or references relating to restricted patients, may sit as President of the Tribunal in those cases.

## 5. Consent to treatment

At common law consent to medical treatment is required, except in a case of urgent necessity. Further the doctor must not be negligent in carrying out the treatment. Civil liability can arise if the doctor has been negligent in treating the patient or if he has not obtained the consent of the patient when he should have done. However, the plaintiff in an action for medical negligence has an uphill task as the definition of medical negligence has been in the hands of the medical profession for a long time. The doctor "is not guilty of negligence if he has acted in accordance with a practice accepted as proper by a responsible body of medical men skilled in that particular art."[12]

The common law principles relating to consent apply equally where the person is a mental patient, except to the limited extent that the Mental Health Act 1983 dispenses with them. Under section 63 of that Act consent is not required for any treatment for the mental disorder from which the patient is suffering except the treatments mentioned in sections 57 or 58 of that Act. Treatments, such as psycho-surgery, can usually only be given with the patient's consent or an independent medical opinion.

As already pointed out:[13] "The consent of a subnormal patient is easily obtained but that does not rob the consent of its validity. Mentally disordered persons should have the right both to give consent to therapeutic procedures and to withhold such consent, unless there are good reasons against this."

At one time it was thought that where a mental patient refused consent to treatment, an application could be made to have him admitted to hospital for treatment, under section 3 of the Mental Health Act 1983, for one night and then to give him leave of absence under section 17 of the 1983 Act. It was considered that this device could be used solely for the purpose of compelling the patient to submit to treatment where the doctor believed that it was the treatment which kept the patient well and out of hospital. Mental Health Review Tribunals agreed with this view and refused to use their power under section 72 of the 1983 Act to discharge the patient in those circumstances.

Section 72 provides that the tribunal is obliged to discharge the patient if satisfied that he is not then suffering from mental illness of a nature or degree which makes it appropriate for him to be liable to be detained in hospital for medical treatment. The tribunals held that the phrase "liable to be detained" could be interpreted as giving them power not to discharge someone who did not need to be in hospital at the time of leaving but who might need to be re-admitted at short notice.

However, in *R. v. Hallstrom*[14] it was held that although section 3 of the 1983 Act gave authority for a patient to be admitted to hospital for treatment and detained there, such "admission for treatment" was restricted to treatment in hospital as an in-patient and did not extend to out-patients whom it was intended to admit and detain for a purely nominal period during which no necessary treatment would be given. Section 3 could not be used for attaching conditions to out-patients.

Thus apart from specific instances, where consent to treatment is dispensed with under the 1983 Act, the ordinary common law rules apply to mental patients. That is to say, no treatment should be given unless the patient consents, either expressly or implicitly, or treatment is for the prevention of harm to himself or others; or, in very limited circumstances, in cases of necessity. For example, in the case of an unconscious road accident victim or if during an operation to which the patient has consented, it is discovered that further treatment in urgently required. Unless these principles are adhered to, those giving the treatment could be liable in either negligence or trespass.

In *T. v. T. and Another*[15] it was held that although an operation for terminating the pregnancy of a severely mentally handicapped woman aged 19, with a mental age of about 3, without consent was tortuous, the court in exercise of its discretion, granted a declaration that the operation was lawful in the circumstances. In doing so, the court accepted that there was no one, such as a guardian, who could give consent to the operation, under the Mental Health Act 1983, and that consent could not be implied, as the patient could never in fact give consent on her own behalf. The Mental Health (Amendment) Act 1982 reduced the powers of the guardian to the "essential powers" and placed the patient in the same position as informal patients in relation to consent to treatment. Nor did the court have the former jurisdiction of the Crown as parens patriae.

In *R v. Berkshire Health Authority*[16] the House of Lords held that at common law a doctor could lawfully operate on, or give other treatment to, adult mental patients incapable of consenting, provided that the operation, or other treatment was in the best interests of such patients. The lawfulness of a doctor operating on, or giving treatment to, an adult patient disabled from giving consent would depend not on any approval or sanction of a court, but on the question whether the operation or other treatment was in the best interests of the patient concerned. However, the Law Lords went on to add that, in practice, an application should be made to court for a declaration that the operation was in the best interests of the patient, before sterilizing a mentally incompetent adult woman to avoid any risk to her of pregnancy.

## 6. Consent to treatment under the Mental Health Act

By far the most controversial part of the 1982 Act was that dealing with the treatment in hospital of patients detained under the Act. Speeches during the debates[17] varied from those advocating no treatment at all without consent to those who advocated that any treatment should be given without consent. In the result, provisions were enacted which allow most forms of treatment to be given without consent, some to be given only with consent and some only after a second opinion has been obtained. The newly established Mental Health Act Commission was given general supervisory and protective powers over detained patients.

These provisions were long overdue but successive Governments were reluctant to tackle the problem. The traditional view was that if the law allowed compulsory detention in hospital, it could hardly interfere in the clinical relationship in hospital.[18]

The consent provisions apply to any patients liable to be detained under the Mental Health Act, except those admitted under the short term powers, including those remanded to hospital for report. Restricted patients, who are conditionally discharged are not subject to the provisions relating to consent to treatment. (See now section 56(l)(c) of the 1983 Act). They are therefore dealt with as if they were informal patients. That is, generally speaking, consent is required under the ordinary common law principles, except in cases of necessity. Under section 49 of the 1982 Act (now section 63 of the 1983 Act) the consent provisions apply only to treatment for mental disorder under the direction of the Responsible Medical Officer. They do not apply to other treatments given solely for physical disorders, where the common law principles apply.

## 7. Treatment requiring consent and second opinion

Under section 43 of the 1982 Act (now section 57 of the 1983 Act) surgical operations destroying brain tissue, or destroying the functioning of brain tissue, and forms of treatment specified in regulations made by the Secretary of State for Health, require not only consent of the patient but a second opinion as well.

Under section 53 of the 1982 Act (now section 118 of the 1983 Act) the Code of Practice must specify treatments which give rise to special concern, in addition to those specified by regulations. It is extraordinary that although several drafts have been produced[19] the current Code was not laid before Parliament until December 1989 and published in May 1990.

The second opinion has to be given by a medical practitioner (not being the Responsible Medical Officer) and two other persons (not being doctors) each appointed by the Mental Health Act Commission on behalf of the Secretary of State.[20] The three persons so appointed must certify in writing that the patient is capable of understanding the nature, purpose and likely effects of the treatment and has consented to it.  Additionally the medical practitioner must certify in writing that, having regard to the likelihood of the treatment alleviating or preventing a deterioration of the patient's condition, the treatment should be given.   Before giving the certificate, the medical practitioner must consult two other persons who have been professionally concerned with the patient's medical treatment, one of whom is a nurse, and the other either a nurse or a doctor.

## 8.  Treatment requiring consent or second opinion

Section 44 of the 1982 Act (now section 58(1) of the 1983 Act) provides that such forms of treatment, as are specified by the Secretary of State in regulations, and the administration of medicine, subject to exceptions, if more than three months have elapsed since the medicine was first administered, require, either the consent of the patient, or a second opinion. The three month period can be varied by the Secretary of State by order.

The Responsible Medical Officer is required to furnish reports to the Mental Health Act Commission on the treatment and the condition of the patient when treatment is given under sections 43 or 44 (now sections 57 or 58 of the 1983 Act respectively).  The consent of the patient must be confirmed by the certificate of the Responsible Medical Officer, or a medical practitioner appointed by the Secretary of State, stating that the patient is capable of understanding the nature, purpose and likely effects of the treatment and has consented to it.

The second opinion must be given by a medical practitioner (not being the Responsible Medical Officer) appointed by the Mental Health Act Commission, on behalf of the Secretary of State, certifying in writing that the patient is not capable of understanding the nature, purpose and likely effects of the treatment or has not consented to it but that, having regard to the likelihood of its alleviating or preventing a deterioration of his condition, the treatment should be given.  As with section 43 (now section 57 of the 1983 Act), before giving the certificate the practitioner is required to consult two other persons who have been professionally concerned with the patient's treatment. One of whom is a nurse and the other a nurse or a doctor.

In *R. v. Mental Health Act Commission Ex parte W.*[21] it was held that the subcutaneous injection of small cylindrical implant to treat the patient's sexual deviancy was not a surgical operation within the meaning of section 57 of the 1983 Act and the Commissioners therefore had not power to refuse the course of treatment. Regulation 16(l)(a) of the Mental Health (Hospital, Guardianship and Consent to Treatment) Regulations 1983 requires a certificate from the Commissioners under section 57 of the 1983 Act for "the surgical implantation of hormones for ... reducing male sexual drive." The applicant was a man of 27 and a compulsive paedophile with several convictions for indecency with young boys. Stuart-Smith L.J. said that "in ordinary common parlance, an injection by a conventional hypodermic syringe would not be described as 'surgical implantation.'"

Under section 45 of the 1982 Act (now section 59 of the 1983 Act) the consent or certificate can relate to a plan of treatment where the patient is to be given one or more forms of treatment. This provides a good deal of flexibility as the plan can specify, either the circumstances under which a particular treatment is to be given, or the period of time during which it will apply. It can relate to more than one treatment. Under section 46 of the 1982 Act (now section 60 of the 1983 Act) the consent can be withdrawn, except in cases of urgent necessity.

## CHAPTER 6: HOSPITAL ORDERS UNDER 1983 ACT

### 1. Requirements for hospital orders

Under section 37 of the Mental Health Act 1983, where the conditions mentioned in the section are satisfied, it is for the court to decide whether a hospital order is the most suitable method of disposing of the case. This appears to give the court a wide discretion.

However, the discretion is not as wide as it appears because one of the conditions to be satisfied under section 37(4) of the Act is that the psychiatrist, who would be in charge of the patient's treatment, or some other representative of the managers of the proposed hospital, has to give written or oral evidence that arrangements have been made for the admission of the defendant to that hospital within 28 days, in the event of a hospital order being made by the court.

There is no obligation on the psychiatrist, or other representative of the hospital, to make such arrangements. It is entirely at his discretion whether he does so or not. Thus, in practice, the overriding discretion, as to whether a hospital order is made or not, is firmly in the hands of the receiving psychiatrist. It is only when he is willing to accept the defendant as a patient and provide a hospital place for him, that the court can make a hospital order.

Under section 37 the Crown Court can make a hospital order, authorising the admission of the offender to a hospital specified in the order, or a guardianship order only when:

(1) a person is convicted of an offence punishable with imprisonment, unless the sentence is fixed by law;

(2) the court is satisfied that the offender is suffering from mental illness, psychopathic disorder, severe mental impairment or mental impairment, of a nature or degree which makes it appropriate for him to be detained in hospital for medical treatment; and

(3) in the case of psychopathic disorder or mental impairment (the minor disorders) the court is satisfied that detention in hospital for medical treatment is "likely to alleviate or prevent a deterioration of his condition;" (see section 37(2)(a)(i)), or in the case of an

offender who has attained the age of 16 years, the mental disorder is of a nature or degree which warrants his reception into guardianship. (See section 37(2)(a)(ii)).

Even where all three conditions above are satisfied, the court still has to consider whether it is of the opinion, having regard to all the circumstances, including the nature of the offence and the character and antecedents of the offender and to the other available methods of dealing with him, that a hospital order is the most suitable method of disposing of the case. (See section 37(2)(b)).

This immediately suggests that if there is an alternative method of disposing of the case, for example, without taking away his liberty, especially where there is no significant risk to the public, the court would have to consider that alternative and whether it is not a more suitable way of disposing of the case.

Under section 37(3) a magistrates' court may make a hospital order, in any case where the offence is punishable on summary conviction with imprisonment in similar circumstances to those applying in the Crown Court. But, in the case of mental illness and severe mental impairment, the magistrates' court can do so without convicting the offender if it is satisfied that the offender did the act or made the omission with which he is charged.

In *R. v. Lincoln (Kesteven) Justices ex parte O'Connor*[1] the Divisional Court went even further to decide that where the defendant's mental disorder prevented him from consenting to summary trial, the justices could still make a hospital order without convicting the defendant. The justices had taken the view that since the defendant could not consent to summary trial they had to proceed as examining justices. Lord Lane C.J. said that under section 60(2) of the 1959 Act (now section 37(3) of the 1983 Act) no trial was called for. It was the type of case in which Parliament must have contemplated the justices having such a power.

*R. v. Ramsgate Justices ex parte Kazmarek*[2] went a step further in deciding that even where the defendant had elected trial by jury, the justices still had power to make a hospital order as they could do so without convicting the defendant.

Where the justices make an order without convicting, the defendant has, under section 45(1) of the 1983 Act, the same right of appeal as if there had been a conviction.

As illustrated by *R. v. Hatt*[3] there does not have to be a causal connection between the mental disorder and the commission of the offence. In that case, the appellant was convicted of taking and driving away a motor-lorry and of dangerous driving, and made subject to a hospital order and a restriction order, without limit of time. He had previous convictions concerning motor vehicles. The medical evidence was to the effect that he was suffering from a psychopathic disorder and the Munchausen syndrome, as a consequence of which he repeatedly sought admission to hospitals in order to undergo unnecessary operations.

Streatfield J. said that he appeared to have an uncontrollable impulse to take and drive away lorries and a mental affliction, which had caused him to enter hospitals on hundreds of occasions and to undergo a number of unnecessary operations. It had been argued that it was wrong to take this mental affliction into account because it was not related to his urge to take motor vehicles. But section 60 of the 1959 Act (now section 37 of the 1983 Act) did not state that there had to be a connection between the illness and the offence committed. The order had been properly made and the application for leave to appeal was refused.

## 2. Medical recommendations

In order to be satisfied that the offender is suffering from one of the forms of mental disorder mentioned in the Act, the court needs the written or oral evidence of two medical practitioners. What is more under section 37(7) of the 1983 Act, the two practitioners have to agree on the category of disorder and one of them has to be a practitioner, who has been approved by the Secretary of State.

Under section 37(4) of the 1983 Act the court cannot make a hospital order without the consent of the hospital managers, who are the Regional Health Authority, or the Secretary of State for Health, in the case of those needing to be detained under conditions of security. The hospital managers are under no obligation to provide a place in hospital if an order is made. They are usually represented in court by one of their consultant psychiatrists.

Section 37(4) goes beyond the equivalent section in the 1959 Act[4] by requiring the court to be satisfied as to the arrangements of the offender's admission to hospital only on the written or oral evidence of the practitioner who would be in charge of his treatment or another hospital representative. This clearly implements the views of the Butler Committee[5] that it was essential that the consent of the receiving doctor should be obtained before any order is made.

Although one or two witnesses had suggested to the Butler

Committee that local psychiatric hospitals should be required to accept mentally disordered offenders, provided only that they had a bed available, the Committee did not accept this view. They thought that it was not unreasonable that consultants should establish criteria for selecting patients for treatment and that they would act "in the interests of their staff and other patients." This appears to avoid answering the question of what is in the interests of the mentally disordered offender himself, which is, after all, what section 37 is all about and indeed that was the Committee's terms of reference.

Although the Home Secretary is not under any statutory obligation to obtain the consent of the receiving hospital before making a transfer direction under sections 47 and 48 of the 1983 Act, in practice he does not give such direction without the consent of the receiving hospital. This has always been the practice[6] although some psychiatrists have disputed it and complained to the Butler Committee that their consent had not been obtained before a transfer direction had been made. This was probably due to lack of communication between the Regional Health Authority and the psychiatrist in question rather than a failure on the part of the Home Secretary to obtain the consent of the hospital.[7]

The Royal College of Psychiatrists had suggested that no hospital order should be made unless the receiving doctor had given evidence to the court. The Butler Committee did not accept this[8] on the ground that it might be inconvenient if the doctor was in a distant hospital and was prepared to receive the patient without having seen him personally. Even this view appears to have been taken to suit the convenience of the doctor rather than the interests of the patient.

However, what is even more surprising is the Butler Committee's refusal to accept that there should be a requirement that the second medical recommendation should be independent of the first, as is required even for civil procedures for compulsory admission under section 12(3) of the Mental Health Act 1983. Indeed originally under section 43 of the Lunacy Act 1890 a medical practitioner who had signed a certificate upon which a reception order had been made was disqualified from being the regular professional attendant of the patient while he was detained under the order. Further, under section 29 of the 1890 Act, where two medical certificates were required each medical practitioner had to have examined the alleged lunatic separately from the other and could not be on the staff of the same institution.

The Butler Committee did not think that the case for insisting on a second recommendation, which was independent of the first, was sufficiently strong to outweigh the difficulties which in some cases this could have caused.[9] Thus it is possible under section 37 for the required recommendations to be made by a consultant psychiatrist and his registrar, which surely defeats the whole object of requiring two doctors to give evidence, since it will in practice be difficult for the registrar, as a student of the consultant, to disagree with his assessment.[10]

The reason given by the Butler Committee for not insisting on an independent second recommendation was that it would not always be possible to obtain a second medical recommendation from someone independent of the particular hospital or psychiatric centre, the consultants of which might belong to the hospital. However, the committee recommended that where the hospital order is opposed by the defendant, then, in practice it would be desirable for the recommending doctors to pay due regard to the provisions of what is now section 12(4) of the 1983 Act and to the principle which underlies them. It is hardly satisfactory not to make the provisions of section 12(4) mandatory when one is dealing with the disposal of a criminal case.

It also seems peculiar that there should be this statutory distinction between the medical recommendations required for civil commitment and the recommendations required for commitment by the court in a criminal case. If there was a justification for this difference, and the Butler Committee could not see any reason for this anomaly,[11] one would expect it to be in favour of an accused person rather than someone liable to civil commitment. Although collusion may not be very likely[12] and the recommendations are subject to scrutiny in court, nevertheless, there does not seem to be any possible reason for not putting mentally disordered offenders at least on as favourable a footing as those liable to civil commitment.

Even where the two recommendations are made by psychiatrists who are independent of each other, it is easy for the hospital psychiatrist not to agree with the diagnosis and recommendation of the other psychiatrist, if he does not wish to receive and treat the patient at his hospital. Therefore, it is difficult to find any cases where the inability of the court to make a hospital order can be attributed solely to the lack of a hospital place.

An illustration of this is the unreported case of *R. v. Tinto*, who was tried at the Central Criminal Court during 1984. No hospital order could be made although Tinto suffered from mental disorder. He had sexually assaulted a young girl and was diagnosed as suffering from mental illness and recommended for a hospital order under section 37 of the 1983 Act. The psychiatrist, treating him at an ordinary hospital, also recommended that he was not suitable for treatment there, but should be detained at a Special Hospital. The second psychiatrist did not agree with the diagnosis or that a Special Hospital was necessary. Thus no hospital order could be made although clearly Tinto was mentally ill, as the two psychiatrists could not agree. He was sentenced to seven years' imprisonment.

This case may lend some support to the view expressed in the Butler Report and elsewhere[13] that psychiatrists do not always give their opinions on purely medical matters, but take into account the availability of beds and whether the nursing staff are prepared to look after the offender.

One can understand the reasons behind the provisions of section 37(4), requiring the evidence of the psychiatrist who would be in charge of the patient's treatment. Obviously if he agrees to treat the patient willingly, the chances of success are much greater than if he is expected to treat the patient on the basis of someone else's diagnosis, with which he does not necessarily agree. However, giving, in effect, a right of veto to this one individual seems a very high price to pay for his professional independence at the expense of the treatment of the patient, who may finish up with a long prison sentence, rather than being treated in hospital.

## 3. Suggested improvements to the hospital order provisions

Apart from introducing a requirement for the second medical recommendation to be independent from the first, a far more fundamental amendment is needed, which is even more pressing. It is to impose a duty on the Secretary of State for Health or the Regional Health Authority, as the case may be, to provide a hospital place once a hospital order has been made. This would hardly be a revolutionary change as local authorities already have a duty imposed on them under section 65 of the Housing Act 1985 to secure that accommodation is made available for the occupation of any homeless person, subject to certain conditions upon which the authority has to be satisfied. Even hospital managers are obliged to find a hospital place where a person is found to be unfit to plead or is found to be not guilty by reason of insanity.

When the House of Commons debated the issue as to whether hospitals should be compelled to admit an offender who was made the subject of a hospital order by a court, the proposal to do so was defeated, not on its merits, but due to a Parliamentary convention.[14]

The vote on the issue was tied and by convention the Speaker or the Chairman of a Committee of the House always casts his vote in favour of the status quo. Thus the amendment to compel hospitals to provide places where a hospital order had been made was defeated.

Section 39 of the Mental Health Act 1983 is quite inadequate for remedying these shortcomings in that Act.[15]

It simply empowers a court, wishing to make a hospital order, to require the Regional Health Authority to furnish information about hospitals where arrangements could be made for the admission of the offender.

The inadequacy of this provision is illustrated by *R. v. Harding*[16] where Lord Justice Lawton said that "anyone who obstructed the execution of an order or procured others to obstruction might be guilty of contempt of court." However, firstly usually the hospital psychiatrist would simply refuse to agree to the opinion of the other psychiatrist with the result that no hospital order could be made; his medical diagnosis could hardly be said to be obstruction; and in any case, it would be very difficult to show that he had been unreasonable in his opinion, if, for instance, he said that the offender suffered from mental impairment rather than severe mental impairment. Secondly, the making of satisfactory arrangements for the offender's admission to hospital is a condition precedent to the making of the order. Thus the failure of the hospital managers to make a bed available could not obstruct the execution of the order.

Section 39 is hardly a sufficient safeguard. In the interests of justice and to restore the real decision making power to the court, neither of the psychiatrists should be connected with the prospective receiving hospital but could be chosen, for instance from an independent panel of psychiatrists, approved by the Home Office, in view of the Department of Health's existing obligations for providing places at the Special Hospitals so that there would be no conceivable conflict of interest. Or better still by the Mental Health Act Commission who already appoint psychiatrists under section 121(2)(a) of the 1983 Act in connection with the consent to treatment provisions of that Act. This would mean that the diagnosis of the offender's mental disorder would be far more impartial and the consideration, of whether a hospital bed was available or not at a particular hospital, would not be the determining factor in the making of a hospital order.

Thus the court would make its decision under section 37 on the basis of all available evidence, including non-medical evidence, as to whether a hospital order is the most suitable method of disposing of the case. If so, the court could then decide, having regard to the nature of the offence and the character and antecedents of the offender, the category of the hospital to which the patient should be admitted. That is to say, the degree of security which would be needed in the public interest. Thereupon it would become the duty of the responsible Regional Hospital Authority or the Secretary of State for Health to provide a place at the type of hospital specified in the order.

It could be argued that the specifying of the category of hospital in the order could be a retrogressive step, as one of the achievements of the Mental Health Act 1959 was its flexibility in not tying any particular class of patient to any particular category of hospital. However, the court already has to name a specific hospital in the order. The only way that the specified hospital can be changed is under section 37(5), if by reason of an emergency or other special circumstances it is not practicable for the patient to be received into the hospital specified in the order.

If instead of naming the specific hospital the court was required simply to specify the category of hospital, it would be an improvement on the present system by making it more flexible and far less rigid. Most important of all, it would not leave these decisions solely in the hands of psychiatrists, who already have sufficient involvement in making the diagnosis and undertaking the treatment of the patient.

None of these suggestions is intended as a criticism of psychiatrists, who are without doubt dedicated and highly professional individuals devoted to acting in the best interests of their patients. However, they are sometimes put in an impossibly difficult situation under the present system, when they are unable to concentrate on purely medical matters and are distracted by financial and managerial responsibilities. The system of hospital orders should be so organised that justice is seen to be done and possible conflicts of interests removed, without in any way implying that under the present system psychiatrists act other than in the best interests of justice.

## 4. Hospital order cases

Occasionally it happens that the court itself is not satisfied of the suitability of the hospital place offered to the offender. This happened in *R. v. Morris*.[17] Morris had murdered his wife of 72 who had been seriously ill. In many ways it could be classed as a mercy killing. He was convicted of manslaughter on a plea of diminished responsibility and sentenced to life imprisonment.

Jones J. refused to allow the prosecution to tender rebutting evidence of insanity during the trial. But there was prosecution evidence that the defendant's mental illness might be worse than that spoken of by his own doctors. There was also evidence that the defendant could be admitted to a local hospital, but no evidence was given that a place was available for him at a special hospital. The judge in sentencing Morris said that he was not sure that the defendant's mental health was not worse than that of diminished responsibility and that he was not going to have the responsibility of setting him anywhere near liberty but would pass such a sentence as would involve him being in the hands of the Secretary of State who had power to send him to the right place.

The Court of Criminal Appeal held that where punishment was not intended and the sole object of the sentence was that the defendant should receive mental treatment, section 60 of the Mental Health Act 1959 required that powers under that section should be used and the matter should not be left to be dealt with by the Home Secretary under section 72 of that Act. Lord Parker C.J. went on to say that in the special circumstances of the case the judge was right to leave the matter entirely to the Secretary of State by sending the defendant to prison.

It is difficult to see what special circumstances warranted a life imprisonment on a man, who was obviously mentally ill. The circumstances are certainly not satisfactorily explained in the judgement of Lord Parker. Philip Morris had killed his wife to prevent her suffering. He was hardly likely to kill any one else. Further, it was not explained why a hospital order was not made coupled with a restriction order under section 65 of the Mental Health Act 1959. If that had been done, in those days Morris' discharge would still have been at the discretion of the Home Secretary on the advice of a Mental Health Review Tribunal. The judge himself admitted that "maybe prison is not the right place for you... " but yet proceeded to pass sentence of life imprisonment without even considering a restriction order.

A restriction order was referred to by the defendant's counsel: "The inference from the evidence is that the appellant is not a danger to the public, and the judge could have achieved his object better by making a hospital order under section 60 together with a restriction order under section 65."

Also there is no explanation why the judge himself did not make enquiries as to the availability of a place at a Special Hospital. It is difficult to understand on what grounds the judge did not accept the psychiatrists' view that Morris' condition was suitable for treatment at the local hospital where a place was available. Further, the judge appears to have confused the degree of the defendant's illness with the degree of his dangerousness. It is a 'non sequitur' to say that simply because someone is suffering from more than diminished responsibility or is even insane within the McNaghten Rules, that he can never be treated at a local hospital. This would run counter to the whole philosophy of the Mental Health Act 1959.

*R. v. Morris* leaves a nasty taste as there are so many unexplained loose ends. One is driven to ask whether it is just possible that as the Mental Health Act 1959 had come into force only on 1st November 1960, the courts in 1961 were not familiar with its mechanics. This hardly seems credible in a case involving the Lord Chief Justice and the Attorney General, who appeared as 'amicus curiae' and explained section 60 of the 1959 Act. He only made a brief reference to section 65 of the Act without explaining it. He simply stated that "even where there is a restriction order the offender may be released at any time by the Secretary of State." But surely the Secretary of State would release the offender only when he was satisfied, on adequate medical evidence, that he was cured and no danger to the public.

In *R. v. Cox*[18] the Court of Appeal was able to put matters right by varying the sentence of life imprisonment for manslaughter, based on diminished responsibility, to a hospital order coupled with a restriction order under section 65 of the 1959 Act. The trial judge seems to have referred only to section 72 of the 1959 Act and left the matter with the Home Secretary, following *R. v. Morris*. As Winn L.J. said "but it seems probable that he looked at the summary of MORRIS contained in Archbold (36th edition) at paragraph 718, which does not bring out the particular feature of the case of MORRIS that there was at the time when sentence was passed in that case by the late Austin Jones J., no available safe hospital to which he could have sent this man." This does not increase one's confidence in the judiciary as it seems doubtful whether even by 1967 all the judges fully understood the operation of the Mental Health Act 1959.

*R. v. McFarlane*[19] goes some way towards restoring one's faith in the judiciary. In that case Scarman L.J. pointed out that some interim accommodation was needed between an open hospital and a Special Hospital; indeed, the sort of accommodation specified by the Butler Committee, which is referred to in the judgement. In the absence of such accommodation the Court of Appeal substituted a hospital order, specifying Rampton Special Hospital, with a restriction order.

It is interesting to note that by the time of the Second Reading of the Mental Health (Amendment) Bill in the House of Commons[20] there were places in all but one of the regional health authorities for regional secure units and that by 1985, it was hoped that 500 places would be made available in such units. Not only has this target been achieved but, in fact in 1985 the South East Thames Regional Authority alone opened a 30 bed secure clinic in Bethlem Royal Hospital in South London and four 15 bed secure clinics in Kent, Sussex and Surrey. As stated by the Earl of Dundee (Lords Hansard 7th November 1988, Col. 524) there are now 518 places available in secure units. Although this is much less than that recommended by the Butler Committee, the Department of Health is encouraging the development of more places where needed.

Two cases which have caused particular difficulty in recent years are *R. v. Evans*[21] and *R. v. Porter*.[22] But in spite of all the adverse publicity these cases received in legal journals,[23] the newspapers, television and radio, as explained below, hospital places were eventually found for them.

Both the above cases concerned young women, who were tried by Judge Verney at the Aylesbury Crown Court. Tina Evans had set light to the quilt of her bed in the psychiatric ward of St. John's Hospital near Aylesbury. She spent four months in the psychiatric wing of Holloway Prison, as the Milton Keynes Health Authority could not afford to pay for the girl's treatment in a private psychiatric hospital. It could manage funding for only six months and the psychiatrist, Dr. Peter Grabbett, stated that Tina Evans' treatment could be a very long process. It could take a few years. In spite of all these difficulties, eventually a hospital place was found for Tina Evans at the Moss Side Hospital in Liverpool and the Aylesbury Crown Court was able to make a hospital order after the defendant had spent four months in Holloway Prison.

In *R. v. Porter*, Wendy Porter had set fire to a printing works where she was employed. The medical evidence showed that she suffered from a psychopathic disorder. She was sent to St. Andrews Psychiatric Hospital under a psychiatric probation order made in pursuance of section 3 of the Powers of Criminal Courts Act 1973. A hospital order could not be made as section 37(2)(a)(i) of the Mental Health Act 1983 was not satisfied. That is, the court was not satisfied that medical treatment would be likely to alleviate or prevent the deterioration of her condition.

In April 1984 a Mental Health Review Tribunal recommended that Wendy Porter should not be discharged. In June 1984, however, St. Andrews Hospital discharged her and her behaviour deteriorated.

Within two weeks she breached the conditions of her probation order by causing substantial damage to a car by scratching graffiti on it. She was found by the Police sitting on top of the car, the door handles of which she had tied together.

Placed in a hostel for assessment, Wendy Porter set light to a metal waste-paper bin, absconded frequently, assaulted staff and caused severe disruption. St. Andrews refused to re-admit her as they believed that she would not respond to treatment and they had no secure facilities. In any case, Oxford Regional Health Authority refused to pay for a place for her at St. Andrews Hospital. Bearing in mind that she would be a danger to the public, the court had no alternative to sentencing her to life imprisonment for arson.

Clearly it would not have been appropriate to make a further probation order, in view of the breaches of her previous order. A hospital order could not have been made at the Crown Court as Wendy Porter suffered from a psychopathic disorder and under section 37(2)(a)(i) of the 1983 Act a person suffering from a psychopathic disorder can be subject to a hospital order only if the court is satisfied that medical treatment is likely to alleviate or prevent a deterioration of her condition. In Wendy Porter's case St. Andrews Hospital refused to re-admit her on the express ground that she would not respond to treatment. She had not responded to treatment during the two years she had already been in their care under a psychiatric probation order made under section 3 of the Powers of Criminal Courts Act 1973.

In *R. v. Porter (Wendy)*,[24] on appeal, against a sentence of life imprisonment for arson and criminal damage, the Lord Chief Justice complained just as much about the state of the law of mental health, as well as the lack of suitable places in hospital. He stated:

> "It should be unnecessary for their Lordships' or any other court to have to keep on saying that there were people for whom a special hospital might not be appropriate and prison was certainly inappropriate."

Unfortunately, Wendy Porter's condition deteriorated rapidly in Holloway prison. Her condition became so bad that a reassessment was made of her mental condition, which resulted in a diagnosis that she was suffering from a major mental disorder. Thus, under section 37 of the Mental Health Act, whether the treatment would be likely to alleviate or prevent a deterioration of her condition was no longer a determining factor and the Court of Appeal was in a position to make a hospital order, with a restriction on release without limit of time. The appellant was ordered to be kept in Moss Side Special Hospital.

There is, of course, provision for people for whom a special hospital or prison is not appropriate. It is to be found in section 3 of the Powers of Criminal Courts Act 1973, to which Miss Wendy Porter had already been made subject without success. In her circumstances it was not therefore a viable option. Under that section, the court can make a probation order and include in it a requirement that the offender shall submit, during the whole of the probation period or such part of it as may be specified in the order, to treatment by or under the direction of a duly qualified medical practitioner with a view to the improvement of the offender's mental condition.

*R. v. Porter* illustrates that what is needed is provision of far more "interim secure units," as recommended by the Butler Report almost 20 years ago.[25] Although the recommendation was for an initial target of 2,000 places, many more would be needed today. In 1985 it was alleged that officially only 91 prisoners were detained in prison, who should have been in hospital.[26] In the same year others[27] estimated that some 46,000 or 34 percent of Britain's prison population were mentally disordered.

However the above estimate takes a broad view of mental disorder. It mentions such matters as bedwetting being an indication of mental distress. According to the Earl of Dundee (Lords Hansard 7th November 1988 Cols. 528,530) on 31st March 1988 there were 235 prisoners who were considered to be detainable in hospital. This was 110 fewer than in September 1987. Thus the Government admits that there are people in prison who should be subject to hospital orders had facilities been available.

## 5. Decline in the number of hospital orders

There was a sharp increase in the number of hospital orders under the Mental Health Act 1959. In the last year of the Mental Deficiency Act 1913, 344 offenders had been compulsorily committed to hospitals. But by 1961, the year of the coming into force of the 1959 Act, these increased to 1059 under that Act. In the last year of the operation of the Mental Health Act 1959, that is in 1982, hospital orders had slumped back to 600, the peak having been reached in 1970 with 1438 such orders.

The reason for this decline would seem to be the same as for the decline in the number of persons, who received hospital orders for diminished responsibility manslaughter, by 1982. This is due to the fact that while in the 1960s hospital accommodation was provided for such cases as a matter of course, by the 1970s hospital managers started to decide for themselves whether a hospital place should be provided in any particular case. In the 1990s these hospitals have even tighter budget constraints. These considerations have in turn had the effect on the number of cases recommended for hospital treatment by psychiatrists.

It would seem from *R. v. Higginbotham*[28] that if there is evidence supporting a hospital order and the court is not satisfied about the security of the hospital which has offered a place, it should make inquiries about more secure hospital accommodation and imprison the accused only as a last resort. In *Higginbotham* the accused had a record of stealing motor cars. He was dealt with by a hospital order coupled with a restriction order under sections 60 and 65 of the Mental Health Act 1959 (now sections 37 and 41 of the 1983 Act). He was sent to an ordinary hospital and while there he was let out for a day and he stole a car. He was chased by the Police and collided with a bus thus wrecking the car. He was sentenced to eight years preventive detention.

The Court of Criminal Appeal said that it was unsafe for courts to assume that the making of a hospital order coupled with a restriction order would be sufficient of itself to ensure that the convicted person would be kept in safe custody. The court went on to suggest that apparently the only way in which that result could be achieved was for the court to ascertain first before making an order, which hospital could receive the accused and further find out whether the hospital was one in which facilities existed for keeping patients in safe custody so that they would not have the opportunity to walk out and commit further crimes. There were such institutions and if it was discovered that there was no vacancy in any institution in which the convicted person could be kept in safe custody, one must point out that the powers of the court to make a hospital order were permissive not mandatory.

If the court thought it necessary for the protection of the public that the accused man should be incarcerated, then the court should use its ordinary penal jurisdiction in order that if the prisoner needed medical treatment, arrangements could be made by the Prison Commissioners for such treatment to be given in a place where he could be kept in safe custody and the kind of thing which happened in that case avoided.

In *R. v. Gunnell*[29] the Court of Appeal went as far as to say that sometimes even a secure hospital may not be sufficient for protecting the public. Gunnell had escaped more than twenty times from ordinary mental hospitals and had even been sent to Rampton where he remained until he was released. He was then convicted of several rapes and sentenced to life imprisonment.

The Court of Appeal said that it was true that Rampton was a secure hospital but it did not mean that he would not get away from there. Bearing the interests of the public in mind, the court thought that it was far safer that he should be kept in prison for so long as it was necessary rather than that he should be left to be dealt with as a hospital might deal with him, on a doctor and patient relationship under which it might be considered safe for him to be free, whereas from the public angle he remained a menace.

Thus again in *R. v. Harvey and Ryan*[30] Rosemary Harvey was a prostitute who had killed another prostitute so that she could have possession of the latter's child. Three medical witnesses agreed that she was psychopathic and dangerous. Broadmoor had a vacancy for her if the court made a hospital order. Since her crime had been reduced to manslaughter because of diminished responsibility, the court had discretion whether to make a hospital order or not. The judge refused to do so as the accused might be discharged by the hospital when they could do nothing further to cure her. The ground for this decision was that she could be transferred to hospital if necessary and be transferred back to prison when the hospital could do no more for her.

In *R. v. Greenberg*[31] on the other hand, the Court of Appeal thought that a hospital order coupled with a restriction order without a limit as to time was preferable to a long determinate prison sentence, from the public safety point of view. In that case the appellant had been found guilty of buggery and of indecently assaulting small boys. At the trial there was insufficient evidence for a hospital order. The appellant was sentenced to thirteen years' imprisonment. On appeal, additional evidence was introduced justifying a hospital order. The Court of Appeal substituted hospital and restriction orders on the ground that it would always be dangerous for Greenberg to be released uncured.

## 6. Improvements to medical recommendation requirements

The object of the mental health legislation must be to do justice to the mental offender. No one would dispute this, although it must be added that the interests of the public must also be an object. It is not easy to see how these objects can be achieved if the court is not free to make a hospital order, solely at its own discretion, without the virtual power of veto by the receiving hospital, if the court considers that the offender is suffering from mental disorder within section 37 of the 1983 Act.

As illustrated by the *Tinto Case*, where the proposed receiving hospital refuses to accept the offender, he is sent to prison instead. This does not do justice to the offender nor is it in the public interest, as there is always the possibility that, in cases like Tinto, when the offender is released from prison in about five years, uncured, he would start molesting young girls again.

As happened in *R. v. Magnolia*,[32] a prison sentence, with remission, does not aim to cure the offender, whereas a hospital order's sole object is to treat the offender so that he can be released when cured. In *Magnolia* Judge Hazan said: "The time has now come when matters relating to the parole authorities ought to be seriously looked at. I have now dealt with a persistent sex offender and persistent armed robber who have been released early from sentences and then returned to precisely what they have been up to before." Magnolia was jailed for four years for rape in 1980. He was paroled after 14 months. In March 1982 he was sentenced to 15 months and ordered to serve the remainder of his previous term for indecent assault. The Parole Board freed him in May 1983. Within weeks he was in the Central Criminal Court again for rape. In December 1984 he was jailed for 2 years for indecent assault. He was released on parole in September 1985. He again raped a girl of 19 and this led to Judge Hazan's criticism of the Parole Board and a sentence of life imprisonment for Magnolia.

## 7. Possible breach of statutory duty

One possibility might be to consider whether the Secretary of State's statutory duty under sections 3(1) and 4 of the National Health Service Act 1977 could be enforced by a court. This would be an uphill task as the sections leave so much to the discretion of the Minister. He is obliged to provide hospital accommodation only to such extent as he considers necessary to meet all reasonable requirements.

In English law judicial redress is more readily available for wrongful acts than for wrongful omissions. In view of the lack of effectiveness of the judicial process in obliging a public body to perform its duties, usually the most important remedies are extra-judicial. In certain circumstances a person aggrieved by failure to carry out a public duty may be awarded damages or a declaration or a mandatory injunction or an order of mandamus requiring the authority to perform its public duty. However, the conditions before any of this can happen are so difficult to satisfy that often the only practical method will be political.

This was illustrated by *In Re Walker's Application*[33] concerning the failure of a regional health authority to provide a life saving operation for a baby. The Master of the Rolls said that it had been accepted by the health authority that the National Health Service authorities and the Secretary of State for Social Services were amenable to judicial review where there was reason to believe they might be in breach of their public law duties. Nevertheless it was not for the court to interfere and substitute its own judgement for that of those responsible for the allocation of resources. It would only interfere if there had been a failure to allocate funds in a way which was "reasonable" in the *Wednesbury*[34] sense or where there were breaches of public law duties. Thus although the Court of Appeal did not provide a remedy in this instance, political pressure on the Prime Minister was successful[35] and the operation provided.

The usual position is that anyone who has an immediate personal interest in the performance of a public duty may bring an action for a declaration as to the scope of that duty. More often than not the plaintiff would be awarded a declaration that the defendant had failed to perform his statutory duty although he has not committed a civil wrong that gives the plaintiff any right of action for damages against him.[36]

An action for a mandatory injunction would be available if the plaintiff was entitled to bring an action for damages for breach of duty. Action for mandamus has now become merely of historical interest.[37]

In *Meade v. Harringey L.B.C.*[38] the local authority had committed a breach of statutory duty to keep schools open at the behest of the trade unions. It was held that anyone who suffered special damage by the breach, such as a parent, had a right of action for damages and for an injunction.[39] However, as by the time the appeal was heard the schools had been opened no orders were made.

If Lord Denning's view in *Meade v. Harringey L.B.C.*, that omissions are covered as well as positive acts, was to be upheld by the House of Lords, this case could have an impact on the failure to make arrangements for hospital admissions under section 37, as such failure is often due to pressure put on psychiatrists giving evidence by nursing staff of the hospital and their trade union.[40]

The above analysis suggests that improvements to the present system of hospital orders could be made by relatively modest amendments by imposing a duty on hospital authorities to provide hospital places whenever the court has made a hospital order, on the ground that it was the most suitable method of disposing of the case and thus restoring the effective decision making power to the court and leaving the psychiatrist solely the responsibility for the diagnosis of the patient.

## CHAPTER 7: RESTRICTION ORDERS UNDER THE MENTAL HEALTH ACT 1983

### 1. Requirements for restriction orders

A restriction order imposes limitations on the release of a patient subject to a hospital order. Where the Crown Court has made a hospital order under section 37 of the Mental Health Act 1983, it can also make a restriction order under section 41, which can be either for a limited period or unlimited, if the Court considers that such an order is necessary for the protection of the public from serious harm. In considering whether a restriction order is necessary for this purpose, the court must have regard to the nature of the offence, the antecedents of the offender and the risk of his committing further offences if set at large.

A restriction order can be made only when all the requirements of a hospital order have been met and at least one of the two required medical practitioners has given oral evidence. There is no requirement in section 41 for the court to satisfy itself that the managers of the hospital specified in the order are willing to accept the patient on a restriction order basis.

Nevertheless the Butler Report[1] states that as a matter of good practice the courts should invariably consult the receiving doctor before making a restriction order and that "it should be a statutory provision that the consent of the doctor to accept the patient on these conditions should be required." It was thought that the relevant requirement, to the effect that one of the two doctors should give oral evidence before a restriction order was made, was not good enough as the oral evidence could be that of the Prison Medical Officer and not the receiving doctor.

Fortunately this recommendation was not implemented. As stated in the previous chapter, the psychiatrists already have a much wider role than a purely diagnostic and treatment one. From the psychiatrist's own point of view, as well as the patient's, it would be far preferable for the psychiatrist's role to be limited to purely medical considerations so that the court is given a freer hand in deciding whether to make orders under sections 37 and 41 of the 1983 Act or not.

The reason for the Butler Report's view that the consent of the receiving psychiatrist should be required before the making of a restriction order was that probably psychiatrists would recommend hospital orders in more cases if the possibility of a restriction order being imposed in addition without their agreement were removed.

If this reason given by the Butler Committee is valid, it means that in making their recommendations psychiatrists do not restrict themselves to only relevant considerations. Such as whether the offender is suffering from one of the four forms of mental disorder specified in the Act and whether the disorder is of a nature or degree which makes it appropriate for him to be detained in hospital and, in the case of the minor disorders, whether the treatment is likely to alleviate or prevent a deterioration of his condition.

It is difficult to see how a premature consideration of whether the court is likely to make a restriction order can affect the medical issues regarding the making of the hospital order. Surely it would be better for the psychiatrists to concentrate on these medical issues, so that an order can be made which is in the best interests of the patient.

## 2. Problems with restriction orders

One problem with restriction orders without a time limit is that, as such orders are potentially for life, some offenders are likely to remain in hospital for a great deal longer for a comparatively minor offence than they would have done, if they had been given prison sentences. The theory being that such orders are not for punitive purposes but simply for the benefit of the patient in curing him.

Thus in *R. v. Bennett*[2] the Court of Appeal, rather surprisingly, refused to admit that a hospital order of unlimited duration was more severe than a prison sentence. The appellant had pleaded guilty to two charges of indecent assault and was sentenced to three years' imprisonment. His mental condition was investigated and the Secretary of State made an order, under what is now section 47 of the Mental Health Act 1983, in pursuance of which the appellant was admitted to Broadmoor.

On appeal, it was held that a hospital order was the proper order to make, although this might involve detention for a period longer than the prison sentence imposed by the court below, since the hospital order was a remedial order designed to treat and cure the appellant.

Restriction orders are, in effect, a compromise between ordinary hospital orders, where medical considerations prevail, and prison sentences, where the need to protect the public usually prevails. Such orders can be made only by the Crown Court; but if a magistrates' court thinks that it is the appropriate order to make, it can commit an offender of fourteen or more years of age, under section 43 of the

1983 Act, to the Crown Court for a restriction order to be made. If the Crown Court does not make such an order it can make such other order which the magistrates' court could have made for that offence.

A restriction order imposes restricting conditions on a patient subject to a hospital order. These special restrictions are set out in subsections (3), (4) and (5) of section 41 of the 1983 Act as follows:-

(a) none of the provisions of Part II of the 1983 Act relating to the duration, renewal and expiration of authority for the detention of patients apply. The patient therefore continues to be liable to detention under the hospital order until discharged under Part II or absolutely under sections 2, 73, 74 or 75 of the 1983 Act;

(b) no application can be made to a Mental Health Review Tribunal under section 66 or 69;

(c) the powers under section 17 (leave of absence), under regulations made under section 19 (transfer) and under section 23 (discharge) can be exercisable only with the consent of the Secretary of State;

(d) the powers of the Secretary of State to recall the patient under section 17 and to take him into custody and return him under section 18 can be exercisable at any time;

(e) a hospital order does not cease to have effect under section 40(5) - that is to say, where a subsequent hospital order is made;

(f) the Responsible Medical Officer has to examine the patient and report to the Secretary of State at such intervals of not more than twelve months as he may require.

Under section 41(1) of the 1983 Act the special restrictions imposed under that section may be either without limit of time or apply during such period as is specified in the order.

In *R. v. Gardiner*[3] the Court of Appeal ruled that courts should have compelling reasons if they do not impose restrictions under section 41 of the Mental Health Act 1983, when making a hospital order under section 37 of that Act, in cases of crimes of violence or more serious sexual offences. In particular, where there is a record of such offences or a history of mental disorder. About a quarter of all hospital orders made contain restrictions.

The Butler Report[4] endorsed the ruling in *R. v. Gardiner* on the ground that since in most cases the prognosis can not be certain, the safer course was to make any restriction order unlimited in point of time. The only exception being where doctors are able to assert confidently that recovery will take place within a fixed period when the restriction order can properly be limited to that period.

In theory, restrictions can be imposed for a limited period. However, as, unlike prison sentences, they are not designed to reflect the gravity of the offence but to ensure that the patient is not released until it is safe to do so, restrictions are usually without a time limit.

There is no way of predicting when the offender will be cured and thus when it would be safe to release him. The Home Secretary has power to direct that the restrictions be lifted under section 42(1) of the 1983 Act, if he is satisfied that they are no longer necessary. The authority to detain continues automatically while the restrictions last, and the need for periodical renewal under section 20 of the Act does not apply.

Under section 42(2) of the 1983 Act the Home Secretary has power to discharge a patient subject to conditions. Section 41(3)(b) provides that no application can be made to a Mental Health Review Tribunal in respect of a restricted patient under section 66 or 69(1) of the Act.

Although the average period of detention was four and a half years in 1974, one must not overlook the fact that a hospital order coupled with a restriction order without a limit of time is potentially for life,[5] and possibly for a longer period than a life imprisonment may involve. A restricted patient, without a limit on his release, could be detained literally until he dies unless in the meantime the Responsible Medical Officer can state that he has been cured. In which case, if a Mental Health Review Tribunal also find that he no longer suffers from mental disorder, then they have an obligation to release the patient.

This immediately raises the question as to whether it can be justified to detain some one, who may have committed a relatively minor offence, such as theft of a bottle of milk or of a box of tomatoes or indecently exposed himself,[6] involving no violence or serious harm to any body, for a potentially longer period of detention than, say a murderer. Especially as a person who was not mentally ill would probably have received a non-custodial sentence or perhaps a very short prison sentence for such offences.

The Percy Committee had recommended that a restriction order should be made only where a serious offence was involved.[7] However, the legislation, now to be found in section 41 of the 1983 Act imposes no such requirement. Indeed, it does not even refer to violence. Thus restriction orders are regarded as both a means of treating and curing the offender and at the same time as a means of protecting the public.

The Percy Committee's intention was to meet the criticism that patients who had committed sexual or violent crimes were being discharged prematurely and committed similar crimes again. Thus restriction orders were designed to protect the public from what were perceived to be psychiatrists' mistaken opinions that someone had been cured and could be safely discharged, when he had not been cured or was liable to have a relapse. However, it is doubtful if they ever achieved this end as illustrated by cases like *Higginbotham*.[8]

Before 1982 only the Home Secretary could discharge a restricted patient. The matter was in his sole discretion even where the Responsible Medical Officer thought that the patient no longer suffered from mental illness, as illustrated by *Kynaston v. Secretary of State for the Home Department*.[9]

In *Kynaston's Case* the applicant had been sent to Broadmoor under a hospital order, with a restriction order, unlimited in time. The Responsible Medical Officer reported that the patient was no longer suffering from mental illness and recommended his absolute discharge. The advisory board was of the opinion that he remained a manipulative psychopath. It was held by the Court of Appeal that the judge had been right to refuse the applicant leave under section 141 of the 1959 Act to institute proceedings against the Secretaries of State for the Home Department and for Social Services for detaining the applicant after the receipt of the Responsible Medical Officer's report. The applicant could not show that there had been bad faith or a lack of reasonable care, as required by section 141 (now section 139 of the 1983 Act).

If there was doubt about the effectiveness of hospital orders coupled with restriction orders at the time that *Higginbotham's Case* was decided, there is no doubt now that they do not protect the public from mistaken medical opinions. As a result of the change in the law, as a consequence of *X. v. United Kingdom*,[10] the decision regarding the discharge of a restricted patient depends on the opinions of psychiatrists. The Mental Health Review Tribunal has very little discretion once the psychiatrists satisfy the Tribunal that the patient no longer suffers from mental illness.

*X. v. United Kingdom* decided that the release of restricted patients at the sole discretion of the Home Secretary did not amount to a review by a competent court. Article 5(1) of the European Convention On Human Rights provides that "everyone has the right to liberty and security of person. No one shall be deprived of his liberty save in the following cases and in accordance with a procedure prescribed by law." Of the exhaustive list of exceptions in Article 5(1), the relevant sub-paragraph for a mentally ill person is (e), which provides that the detention must be "in accordance with a procedure prescribed by law" and it must be "lawful detention."

This implies that the individual must be shown to be of unsound mind on the basis of objective medical evidence; the mental disorder must be of a kind or degree justifying compulsory detention and the validity of the continued detention must depend on the persistence of the mental disorder. It was decided that the patient should not continue to be held unless there was medical evidence to show that he was still mentally ill and unless this was shown the power of recall of some one who had been conditionally discharged should not arise.

As a result of *X. v. United Kingdom*, the law was amended to allow a restriction order patient to apply to a Tribunal in the period between six months and a year of his detention. (See section 69 of the 1983 Act). Contrary to the trend in the 1982 Amendment Act, of halving the periods before patients could apply to a Tribunal, hospital order patients were the only group to have the period before they could apply to a Tribunal increased. Simply so that restriction order patients should be in no worse position than hospital order patients.

Furthermore, although a Mental Health Review Tribunal must serve notice on the Home Secretary under the Mental Health Review Tribunal Rules 1983 (S.I. 1983 No. 942) where a restriction order patient is involved, the Tribunal is still obliged to release him if he is no longer suffering from mental illness no matter what the Home Secretary's views are regarding the interests of protecting the public from serious harm.

In *R. v. Oxford Regional Health Review Tribunal*[11] the House of Lords upheld an order to quash the Tribunal's decision; one of the grounds being that they had not given the Home Secretary the required notice. In *R. v. Kay*[12] the required notice had been given but to no avail. James Kay had raped a young girl of 12. He was released in April 1986, despite pleas from the Home Office Ministers that he was still a potential danger to the public and should therefore not be released. Shortly after his release he was found guilty of two violent attacks on young women and had to be imprisoned for 6 years.

### 3. Possible amendments of requirements for restriction orders

There is no doubt that restriction orders under section 41 of the 1983 Act are not as effective as they were before 1982 in protecting the public from serious harm. In order to increase the effectiveness of restriction orders it would be necessary to amend section 41. Possibly along the lines of the Government's Consultative Document.[13] That is, where a restriction order had been made and the Mental Health Review Tribunal decided that the patient no longer suffered from mental illness, then instead of the patient being released, he would be sent to prison to serve what would be an adequate sentence commensurate with his offence; the time he had already spent in hospital being of course deducted. However, as announced in Parliament[14] the Government gave up the idea of any amendment of section 41 in the near future.

Oddly enough some time ago, MIND made a similar proposal, along the lines that a restriction order should be more like a transfer direction made by the Home Secretary[15]. MIND's proposal for reform was that either orders of unlimited duration should be limited to specified offences, which involved serious violence, usually carrying a life sentence, as suggested by the Butler Report,[16] or alternatively that the court should make a restriction order for a finite period, commensurate with the offence but at the end of that period the patient should continue to be liable to be detained under a hospital order without restrictions. Under the 1983 Act a Tribunal does not have the power to remove the restrictions and continue the detention of the patient as an ordinary hospital order patient.

The fact that hospital orders coupled with restriction orders are not as effective as they were under the 1959 Act could be an additional factor in the decline of hospital orders in recent years. Previously section 60 and 65 orders meant that the patient would be detained in hospital until the Home Secretary decided it was safe, from the public protection point of view, to release him. The matter was entirely at the discretion of the Home Secretary. But under the present provisions of the 1983 Act a Tribunal is obliged to release the patient if the psychiatric evidence is that he has been cured, no matter what anxieties the Home Secretary expresses from the public safety point of view.

## 4. Restriction order cases

In *R. v. Gardiner*[17] the Court of Appeal summed up the effect of a restriction order in a practice note by stating that when a restriction order is made: -

1. There is authority to detain the appellant for the duration of the order, although the Home Secretary may terminate it at any time if satisfied that it is no longer required for the protection of the public;

2. The patient could only be discharged with the consent of the Home Secretary;

3. The Home Secretary could make the discharge conditional, in which case the patient remained liable to recall during the duration of the restriction order;

4. A patient who was absent without leave could be taken into custody at any time.

This practice note is still probably applicable subject to the modifications, now to be found in the Mental Health Act 1983. That is, under section 73 of that Act a Mental Health Review Tribunal can also discharge a restricted patient and under the 1983 Act the public is entitled to be protected only from "serious" harm. Otherwise section 41 of the 1983 Act more or less repeats the provisions of section 65 of the 1959 Act.

## 5. Cases tried at the Old Bailey during 1984

During an examination of the 23 hospital order cases disposed of at the Central Criminal Court during the first year of operation of the 1983 Act, it was discovered that 13 were coupled with restriction orders. However, it was astonishing to find that in some of these cases where one would have expected to see restriction orders as well, no such orders were made, in spite of the violence involved.

One such case was *R. v. Hurse*, where Barbara Hurse pleaded guilty to unlawful wounding contrary to section 20 of the Offences Against the Person Act 1861. She went to a Barrister's chambers and told the clerk that she wished to see the Barrister about an international law book she alleged that she was writing. When the

Barrister admitted her to his room and she was alone with him, she produced a knife and lunged at him. He grabbed the knife and managed to ward her off. He then called for assistance but by this time his hands were severely lacerated. He lost all feeling in one finger.

The accused admitted that she wanted to kill him. She thought, without any foundation, that she had known him some years prior to the incident. She talked of sexual fantasies on her Jewish American boyfriend and stated that she was tortured by a dye which had been put into her system. The medical evidence showed that she was suffering from mental illness with paranoid and schizophrenic symptoms. She was sentenced to be detained at the Interim Secure Unit, Bethlem Royal Hospital.

It was surprising that such a woman was not made subject to a restriction order under section 41 of the Mental Health Act 1983. It is difficult to understand what possible justification there could be for thinking that she would not be a danger to the public if she were to be discharged prematurely.

In *R. v. Iandolo* again surprisingly there was no restriction order under section 41. Michele Iandolo, who was only 24 years old, attempted to rob a bank. He entered the Bank and threatened the cashier with an imitation firearm and demanded some money. The sub-manager with great presence of mind, managed to stall Iandolo while pretending to collect the cash. In the meantime, he raised the alarm and the Police arrived while he was still in the Bank. As he refused to surrender and he seemed to be dangerous, the Police shot him.

It was found that he was a drug addict and suffered from mental illness. He had delusions that he was being controlled by others and he believed in thought broadcast. He also suffered from persecution complex and third person auditory hallucinations. He was obviously schizophrenic. He was ordered to be detained in Maidstone Hospital under section 37 of the Act. It is possible that no restriction order was made as it was thought that as Iandolo's drug addiction could be cured, once that happened he would no longer be a danger to the public.

Another case where no restriction order was made, perhaps with more justification, was *R. v. Wells*. Paul Joseph Wells set fire to bedding in his hostel cubicle. He was therefore evicted and barred from returning there. He moved to a hotel and due to some disagreement with the Manager of the hotel he set light to the store room. He admitted the offence. The court ordered him to be detained in Horton Hospital in Epsom under section 37 of the 1983 Act. The medical evidence showed that he suffered from mental illness. He was paranoid. He had hallucinations and grandiose ideas such as "his mission being to liberate people from ignorance."

By contrast, in *R. v. Simpson*, Terri Simpson, who had admitted to committing arson, was ordered to be detained in Broadmoor Hospital. A restriction order was also made under section 41 of the 1983 Act without any limit as to time.

In another arson case, however, which seemed just as bad as, if not worse than Simpson, no restriction order was made under section 41 of the 1983 Act. In *R. v. Blair*, George Oswald Blair had a disagreement with a driving school. He set fire to a trail of petrol on their premises causing damage to a staircase. When the Police called at his house to make enquiries, he threatened the three officers with a knife. He pleaded guilty to arson and was ordered to be detained in St. Pancras Hospital. He was diagnosed as suffering from mental illness. He was schizophrenic, paranoid delusions being the major symptom. He believed that people poisoned his food and threatened him through broadcasts on radio and television.

In *R. v. Turner*, again no restriction order was made under section 41 of the 1983 Act, although one would have expected to see one. Geoffrey Turner pleaded guilty to arson endangering lives, contrary to section 1(2) and (3) of the Criminal Damage Act 1971. He lived in the ground floor flat of a converted house. He alleged that two sisters, who lived with their mother on the first and second floors of the same house, laughed at him when they heard him trying to commit suicide. This was quite without foundation, but nevertheless he poured paraffin on their stairs and set light to it. The two sisters had to escape through the first floor window and they were in real danger.

The medical evidence showed that Geoffrey Turner was mentally ill. He suffered from severe schizophrenia, characterised in his case by delusions of persecution, such as that he was being poisoned by neighbours. Turner was sentenced to be detained in Bethlem Royal Hospital.

The above cases are surprising as the court has to consider a restriction order where the protection of the public from serious harm is involved. As already mentioned (page 78), in *R. v. Gardiner* the Court of Appeal stated that judges should have compelling reasons if they did not impose restrictions in cases of crimes of violence or the more serious sexual offences, especially if the offender has a similar record or a history of mental disorder involving violent behaviour. *R. v. Toland*[18] went even further by requiring that there should be a restriction order whenever there was any serious anti-social conduct from which the public required protection, such as repeated burglaries.

Another case, tried at the Old Bailey during 1984 where one would have expected to see a restriction order, was *R. v. Mizon and Darker*. Tracy Ann Mizon was tried with her common law husband, John Cristopher Darker. They were both found guilty of manslaughter, causing grievous bodily harm with intent and cruelty to a person under 16 years of age. The victim being her three year old son, whose father was not Darker. Tracy Mizon alleged that the victim had wet his bed, she lost her temper and punched him in the stomach. She further alleged that the burns on his body were caused by his standing naked in front of a fire. By the time the ambulance arrived to collect the boy, it was found that he had stopped breathing. He had apparently been vomiting. His heart beat was restored in hospital but he had a relapse and died during an operation. The post-mortem examination showed severe bruising and cigarette burns on the body.

The court sentenced Darker to four years' imprisonment but did not sentence Tracy Mizon. Her case was adjourned so that a hospital place could be found for her. In the meantime she was released on bail, on condition that she stayed at the Maudsley Hospital. That hospital could not offer her a place so the case was adjourned a second time.

There followed a dispute between Claybury Hospital and the Royal Free Hospital, as her address in Hornsey, London N8 was on the border between the catchment areas of the two hospitals. Each claimed that the address was served by the other hospital and refused to provide a place. Eventually the North East Thames Regional Health Authority admitted that they were responsible for finding a place in hospital for Tracy Mizon. As no place was available at Friern Hospital, which was the catchment area's psychiatric hospital, they found her a place at St. Andrews Hospital, Northampton. The Authority also undertook to pay for the placement, for six months in the first instance.

It was astonishing that, in the case of Tracy Mizon, not only was no restriction order made but she was even granted bail until a hospital order could be made. Presumably it was thought that as she had no other young children she was not likely to abuse any other child, as she would no longer be under the pressure and responsibility of looking after a young child. Nevertheless in such a case of excessive violence one would have expected to see a restriction order.

In *R. v. Gunnel*[19] for example, it was held that an offender who deserved punishment could be sent to prison, even though he qualified for a hospital order and a suitable hospital place was available. Once the court had decided that treatment in hospital was appropriate, it could go on to consider whether a restriction order under section 41 of the 1983 Act should be made as well.

In *R. v. Gardiner*[20] the Court of Appeal drew attention to the deficiencies of a hospital order on its own without a restriction order, such as that the hospital could discharge the offender at any time and very likely would do so within a year of admission. Further, under the Mental Health Act his detention can not be renewed beyond the initial period, which is now six months under the 1983 Act, unless the medical criteria continue to exist. Once the patient ceases to be liable to detention there is no power to recall him to hospital.

The above unreported hospital order cases disposed of by the Central Criminal Court during 1984 came to light during the author's research of the Old Bailey Papers. They appear to ignore the principles laid down in *R. v. Gardiner*.

## 6. Proposed reforms

Clearly hospital orders coupled with restriction orders are not working satisfactorily as illustrated by the cases considered in section 10 of Chapter 8 (page 101). Patients who have committed offences of violence are being released prematurely when ministers consider them to be a danger to the public. One of the difficulties is that the courts claim that restriction orders are imposed purely for therapeutic purposes (see *R. v. Bennett*[2] ) when they are undoubtedly imposed, not only for the satisfactory medical treatment of the patient, but for the protection of the public as well. It is difficult to deny that additionally they probably have a punitive element. Consequently restriction orders succeed in satisfying none of these ends. The courts recognising this, sometimes try to make up for the deficiency by using the prison system instead, as illustrated by cases such as *R. v. Arrowsmith*.[21]

In spite of what was said in *R. v. Bennett* all courts need to realise that a hospital order coupled with a restriction order is not for purely therapeutic purposes. Once this is recognised, then no doubt, in the interests of justice, courts would try to introduce some sort of proportionality between the seriousness of the offence and the length of the restriction order.[22]

The courts already have the power to impose a restriction order limited in time which could be commensurate with the seriousness of the offence. They very rarely use it, presumably because they regard a restriction order as being imposed for therapeutic purposes and as it is not possible to predict how long it will take before the patient is cured, no time limit is imposed. This ignores the decision of the Court of Appeal in *R. v. Fisher*[23] where the court rightly pointed out that sentences had to be commensurate with the offence in question.

In another case, *R. v. Fish*[24], the defendant had fired a shotgun at a house. He then gave himself up to the Police. He was sentenced to 4 years' imprisonment. The Court of Appeal held that although it was necessary to mark the offence with a severe sentence, it had to be taken into account that the defendant did not intend to shoot anyone. He was acting out of jealousy whilst drunk. The sentence had to be commensurate with the offence. It was therefore reduced to 2 years' imprisonment.

Another outcome of the recognition of the fact that a restriction order is not made for purely therapeutic purposes could be to give the offender a choice of accepting a hospital order and a restriction order or opting for a finite prison sentence.[25] People seem to be under the mistaken impression that a mentally abnormal offender is in all cases incapable of making a choice. That clearly is not so.[26] Furthermore, a mentally abnormal offender's lawyers could explain to him in terms which he could understand what the choice would entail and in really acute cases exercise the choice themselves in the offender's best interests.

Surely, such a system would be better than the present position where the offender has no choice whatsoever and can be detained for long periods for relatively minor offences, which would not normally entail imprisonment or a very short period in prison.[27] An additional advantage of giving the offender a choice would be that as the offender was a more willing patient the chances of his being successfully treated would be greatly enhanced.

So far as protection of the public from serious harm element is concerned, again it is questionable whether restriction orders achieve this end either. Recent cases like *R. v. Pickering*[28] and the Government's Consultative Document,[29] show the public disquiet and lack of confidence in the present system. What is more, the position has been exacerbated now due to severe lack of resources in the staffing and management of hospitals.

It is arguable that if courts accepted the fact that restriction orders were not purely therapeutic and used their power to impose limits of time on such orders commensurate with the offence, hospitals would be more willing to accept hospital order patients. Indeed even in the

1970s psychiatrists were reluctant to recommend hospital orders, for the probably improper, but nonetheless understandable reason, that at a later stage a restriction order could be made without a limit of time without the consent of the hospital.[30]

So far as the third and punitive element of a restriction order is concerned, such orders demonstrably fail again. Their duration has little or nothing to do with the seriousness of the offence. A multiple rapist or even a homicidal maniac could be discharged by a Mental Review Tribunal after a few years, if they were satisfied on medical evidence that he no longer suffered from mental illness.

If the medical evidence was to the effect that the patient no longer suffered from mental disorder, the Tribunal would have no choice but to discharge the patient; no matter what the Home Secretary's views were as to the need to protect the public from the consequences of the premature release of the patient. A Tribunal does not even have the power to remove the restrictions and keep the offender as an ordinary hospital order patient. More flexible powers could be used in monitoring progress for a longer period, on the one hand, or to send him to prison for the rest of what would be a reasonable sentence for the offence, on the other hand. As in fact would happen to transferred patients subject to restrictions and as suggested by the Government's Consultative Document.

The main difficulty with restriction orders, and indeed hospital orders, is the lack of proper definition of mental illness in the Mental Health Act 1983, which means that a great deal is left to medical opinions. Surely mental illness cannot mean, as Lawton L.J. put it in *W. v. L.*[31] what the ordinary sensible man would term "mad." The European Court of Human Rights said in *Winterwerp v. Netherlands*[32] that unsoundness of mind should not include persons solely because their views or behaviour deviate from the prevailing norms. The decision on the question whether a person suffers from mental disorder should be based on objective medical criteria. The Butler Report recommended a definition but unfortunately the 1983 Act did not adopt it as it was thought to be too restrictive.[33]

Even the disorders which are defined are not very clear. For example, "severe mental impairment" is defined as "a state of arrested or incomplete development of mind which includes severe impairment of intelligence and social functioning and is associated with aggressive or seriously irresponsible conduct." "Mental impairment" is defined in exactly the same way except that the impairment of intelligence is required to be "significant" rather than "severe." It is left to the psychiatrists to distinguish between "severe" and "significant." No guidance is given and yet, if the patient suffers from severe mental impairment, a hospital order can be made without the need to show that the condition is treatable and a remand order to hospital for treatment can be made under section 36 of the 1983 Act. If, on the other hand, the offender suffers merely from mental impairment, no hospital order can be made unless the treatment is likely to alleviate or prevent a deterioration of his condition. No remand can be made to hospital for treatment.[34]

In this respect, the 1983 Act took a retrogressive step. Section 4 of the 1959 Act distinguished between "severe subnormality" and "subnormality" by reference to the patient's capacity of living an independent life and guarding himself against serious exploitation in the former case.

The possibility of reforming and co-ordinating the various defences involving mental disorder, such as insanity and diminished responsibility, and the powers of courts to make hospital and restriction orders under the mental health legislation, and ensuring that they meet current needs is considered in Chapter 9. Some of the existing provisions, such as the special verdict have practically fallen into disuse. Others, such as hospital orders decline. Some fundamental reform of the present legislation is long overdue.

CHAPTER 8: MENTAL HEALTH REVIEW TRIBUNALS

## 1. Establishment of Tribunals

Mental Health Review Tribunals were introduced by the Mental Health Act 1959 as independent bodies. They had been recommended by the Percy Commission[1] as a safeguard for long term compulsory patients to balance the Commission's recommendation that judicial commitment should be abolished. Briefly, they provide the opportunity for patients to have their detention reviewed and give a right of appeal should they wish to object to being kept in hospital or under guardianship compulsorily.

The right to appeal to a Tribunal has now been extended to practically all categories of patient suffering from mental disorder, including those admitted for short periods of assessment, and those patients who have a restriction order made against them and those who have been transferred from prison by a direction of the Home Secretary. The extension of this right was due to the decision of the European Court of Human Rights which decided that a writ of habeas corpus may be a sufficient safeguard in an emergency, but it would not be good enough in normal circumstances, as it would not provide a full assessment of the merits of the case.

## 2. Changes included in the Mental Health Act 1983

One of the main changes included in the Mental Health Act 1983 is to give authority to Mental Health Review Tribunals to discharge restricted patients and not simply to advise the Home Secretary to discharge them, as was the position under the Mental Health Act 1959. This was a direct response to the judgement of the European Court of Human Rights in the case of *X. v. United Kingdom*.[2]

Another change was the halving in nearly all cases of the periods, before the expiration of which the detention of patients must be reviewed. New arrangements for the automatic review of a patient's case are also included in the Mental Health Act 1983. The managers of a hospital are required to refer the case of any detained patient who has not exercised his right to make an application to a Tribunal during the three years following his admission to hospital.

Previously legal aid was available for a lawyer only to assist the preparation of a case before a Tribunal. This has now been extended to legal assistance by way of representation before a Tribunal.

## 3. Appointment of members of tribunals

There is a Mental Health Review Tribunal for each of the fourteen National Health Service Regions for England and there is one Tribunal for Wales. The Lord Chancellor is obliged to appoint for each Tribunal legal, medical and lay members. The lay members are appointed after consultation with the Secretary of State for Health. They must have such knowledge or other qualifications as the Lord Chancellor considers suitable.

The medical members as well are appointed after consultation with the Secretary of State for Health and are usually senior consultant psychiatrists. The medical member of the Tribunal is required to examine the patient privately and make any medical inquiries he considers necessary. He may also examine the patient's medical records to form an opinion of his clinical state.

The legal members of Tribunals must have such legal experience as the Lord Chancellor considers necessary. One of the legal members of the Tribunal is the chairman, as provided in paragraph 3 of Schedule 2 to the Mental Health Act 1983. He is responsible for nominating the members of the Tribunal for a particular hearing or class of hearings under the provisions of Schedule 2 to the 1983 Act. His powers include the giving of any direction which may be necessary to secure a "speedy and just determination." Under section 78(6) of the 1983 Act, these functions can be carried out by another member delegated to act if the Chairman is unable to do so.

There are regional Tribunal offices in London, Liverpool and Nottingham, each dealing with several tribunal regions, and one in Cardiff for Wales. The offices are staffed by full time civil servants, who are accountable to the regional Tribunal Chairmen.

For any case, a Tribunal is made up of at least one member from each of the three groups and the lawyer presides, as he can ensure that the proceedings are conducted along traditional judicial lines. However, each member has an equal vote on any questions which arise, including any legal questions. In the case of restricted patients, the presiding legal member must be approved for the purpose under the rules made in pursuance of section 78(4)(a) of the Mental Health Act 1983.[3] Usually circuit judges or recorders are appointed in such cases.

Any member is disqualified from sitting if he is a member or officer of the responsible authority.[4] Thus hospital managers or local social services authority members or officers of the responsible authority can not sit on the Tribunal. Nor can the members or officers of the health authority with which the mental nursing home is registered if the patient is in such a home. It is also a matter of disqualification if the member concerned has any close knowledge of, or connection with, the patient.

However, as decided in *R. v. Oxford Regional Mental Health Tribunal*[5] the Chairman of the Tribunal is not disqualified form sitting on the case of an applicant seeking discharge under section 73 of the Mental Health Act 1983, because he had sat on an earlier application by the same patient. McNeill J., in dismissing an application for judicial review, said that he could not think that at the end of the day any reasonable and fair-minded person sitting in court and knowing of the facts, would have a reasonable suspicion that the applicant would not have a fair hearing. It would be quite wrong to lay down that in the case of a particular application and any successive applications as were permitted, the constitution of the Tribunal or the person presiding had as a matter of law to be changed each time.

## 4. Applications to Tribunal

Patients who are found unfit to plead or found to be not guilty by reason of insanity and admitted to hospital under section 5(1) of the Criminal Procedure (Insanity) Act 1964 are able to apply to a Tribunal within six months of their admission. Patients who have been transferred from prison by the Home Secretary, with or without restrictions, and patients who are subject to a hospital order alone after their period of restriction has come to an end, can all apply within six months of their admission as well.

Under section 56(1)(f) and (2)(b) of the Mental Health Act 1983, those who are subject to hospital orders without restrictions, can apply to a Tribunal once within each period that their detention is renewed. As can those who have been received into guardianship. That is to say, that they may apply once in their second period of six months and thereafter annually.

Although detention of those who are subject to a restriction order does not have to be renewed, nevertheless under sections 70 and 79 of the Mental Health Act 1983 they have the right to apply within equivalent periods as the periods which apply to patients who are not subject to any restriction. Under section 75(2) of the 1983 Act conditionally discharged restricted patients, who have not been recalled to hospital may apply within the second period of twelve months and thereafter bi-annually. There is also an automatic review after each time that a restricted patient is recalled to hospital.

## 5. Automatic reviews

The purpose of an automatic review is to cater for those patients who are incapable of applying to a Tribunal because of their mental state. As well as those who do not realise that they have a right to do so. The hospital managers are obliged to refer to a Tribunal on the expiration of the first six months from the admission of the patient, unless there is a pending reference from the Secretary of State or an application by the nearest relative or an application by the patient following a reclassification. Under section 68(5) of the Mental Health Act 1983 the hospital managers are still required to refer a case if the patient did apply within the first six months of his admission but withdrew his application before it was heard by the Tribunal.

Automatic reviews by hospital managers do not apply to those liable to hospital orders or to those who are transferred from prison. But if the patient is admitted under the Criminal Procedure (Insanity) Act 1964, the Home Secretary is obliged to refer his case to a Tribunal under section71(5) and (6) of the 1983 Act unless the patient has himself applied and not withdrawn his application before it was heard by the Tribunal.

The hospital managers are also obliged to refer to a Tribunal any patient whose detention is renewed and it is more than three years since his case was last considered by a Tribunal. This applies to those patients subject to hospital orders but on whose discharge no restrictions have been made under section 41 of the Mental Health Act 1983. Where the patient is under sixteen years of age the hospital managers must refer his case under section 68(2) of the 1983 Act after the lapse of only one year since his last review.

## 6. References to a Tribunal by the Home Secretary

Where a patient has been conditionally discharged by the Home Secretary or a Tribunal and has been recalled to hospital, the Home Secretary is obliged under section 75(1)(a) of the Mental Health Act 1983 to refer his case to a Tribunal within one month of his return to hospital. This provision is designed to satisfy Article 5(4) of the European Convention on Human Rights. Patients subject to restriction orders can have their case referred to a Tribunal at any time by the Home Secretary under section 71(1) of the Mental Health Act 1983.

Section 77(1) of the 1983 Act provides that no application can be made to a Tribunal except in such cases and at such times as are provided in that Act. Under rule 19 of the Mental Health Review Tribunal Rules (S.I. 1983 No. 942) a patient can request, in writing for his application to be withdrawn if the Tribunal agrees to do so.

Improved access to Mental Health Review Tribunals and easier availability of legal aid for mental patients have had the result of increasing the number of cases heard by Tribunals from 696 in 1978 to 3,168 in 1988.

## 7. Proceedings before the Tribunal

The proceedings are commenced by a written application, signed by the applicant or someone authorised on his behalf. Whenever possible the applicant should include the information set out in rule 3 of the 1983 Rules, such as the patient's address, the address of the hospital where he is detained and the section of the Act under which he is detained. Under rule 4, on receipt of the application, the Tribunal is obliged to send notice of the application to the responsible authority, to the patient, where he is not the applicant and, if the patient is restricted, to the Home Secretary.

It was held by the House of Lords in *Secretary of State for the Home Department v. Oxford Regional Mental Health Review Tribunal and another*,[6] that as the Tribunal had not given the Home Secretary the required notice of the hearing, in breach of the 1983 Rules, the decision could not stand. Lord Bridge said: "My Lords, whatever view be taken, as a matter of construction, of the interaction between sub-sections (2) and (7) of section 73, as to which Woolf J. and the Court of Appeal differed, I find it difficult to see how the Tribunal's decision made in February 1985 can properly stand. Such a fundamental flaw as vitiated the proceedings leading to that decision must surely call for a complete rehearing de novo."[7]

Lord Bridge went on to say that in the interests of justice being seen to be done, the rehearing should be before a differently constituted Tribunal. He pointed out that the purpose of section 73(7) was merely to enable arrangements to be made to satisfy the conditions imposed. Where a conditional discharge was ordered pursuant to section 73(2) of the 1983 Act, which was deferred pursuant to section 73(7) of that Act, the Tribunal were not entitled later to reconsider the question whether the patient should in fact be conditionally discharged. Thus the original decision was final and vitiated by the failure to inform the Home Secretary of the date of the hearing.

*R. v. Yorkshire Mental Health Review Tribunal*[8] also held that where a Tribunal ordered a conditional discharge under section 73(2) of the 1983 Act but deferred it under section 73(7), it could not reconsider its decision. The Tribunal's duty to order conditional discharge under section 73(2) was mandatory and in performing that duty the Tribunal was only concerned with the criteria laid down in section 72(l)(b)(i) and (ii) and nothing outside those provisions.

After the necessary notices have been given, then under rule 6 of the 1983 Rules, the responsible authority is obliged to supply the information set out in Schedule 1 to the Rules within 3 weeks. This information includes matters such as the name and age of the patient, his date of admission to hospital, the name of the health authority maintaining him; the details of the authority detaining him and any later renewals and changes; and the name of the responsible medical officer and the length of time the patient has been in care.

The authority also has to supply an up-to-date medical report on the patient's medical history and current condition, specially prepared for the Tribunal. Finally, the hospital statement must give the views of the hospital managers on the suitability of the patient for discharge. If the patient is a restricted one then the Home Secretary must also supply a statement.

After receiving the statements from the hospital and the Home Office, if applicable, the Tribunal can fix the time and place of the hearing but it must give fourteen days' notice of it to the patient, the applicant, if not the patient, the responsible authority and the Home Secretary, if the patient is restricted.

The Tribunal can send any documents it has received to the patient and the applicant and to the responsible authority unless it considers that the patient's or any one else's health or welfare might be adversely affected. If the Tribunal decides not to disclose any document, it must under rule 12(2) of the Mental Health Tribunal Rules 1983 record its decision in writing.

The Tribunal must always hold a hearing, which must follow the examination of the patient by the medical member of the Tribunal. Under rule 22(3) of the 1983 Rules, at the start of the hearing the presiding member must explain how the Tribunal proposes to proceed. It is usual for the medical member, who has examined the patient, to give his views to the Tribunal before the hearing. However, some Tribunals receive the medical views after the hearing, just before they take a decision.

Neither way is really satisfactory as an opportunity is not given to the applicant or his representative to question those views. Perhaps the lesser evil is for the medical member's report to be presented before the hearing, because although this means that the Tribunal starts the hearing with preconceived ideas, these ideas can come out at the hearing and the applicant has, at least, some opportunity to question them.[9]

The Tribunal sits in private, usually at the hospital where the patient is detained, unless the patient asks for a public hearing and the Tribunal is satisfied that this would not be contrary to his interests. The Tribunal must record its reasons for refusing the patient's request for a public hearing or if, having started a public hearing, it reverts to a private one.

Generally it does not make much difference whether the hearing is private or public. The Tribunal can under rule 21(3) of the Mental Health Review Tribunal Rules 1983 admit any one it likes to a private hearing and exclude any one, whether the hearing is private or public, for all or a part of the proceedings. If it excludes the applicant or patient or their representatives or a representative of the responsible authority, it must record its reasons for the exclusion. Under rule 21(4) and (6) of the 1983 Rules the Tribunal cannot exclude a "qualified" representative of the patient or applicant or a member of the Council on Tribunals.[10]

The patient, the applicant, the responsible authority and any one else who has been notified may attend the hearing and take such part as the Tribunal thinks proper. Under rule 22(1) of the Rules the Tribunal must seek to avoid formality in its proceedings, otherwise it may conduct the hearing in such manner as it considers most suitable, bearing in mind the health and interests of the patient.

The Tribunal is obliged is to hear and take evidence from the applicant, the patient and the responsible authority, who may hear each other's evidence, put questions to each other and call evidence themselves. The Tribunal has power to subpoena witnesses to appear or produce documents and to hear evidence on oath. It is not, however, bound by the ordinary rules of evidence. It can admit evidence which would be inadmissible in a court of law.

Under rule 22 of the 1983 Rules the Tribunal may interview the patient and must do so if he so requests. Such interview may take place in the absence of anyone if the patient so requests. The representative of the responsible authority is usually asked to leave while the patient is being interviewed. Obviously a doctor who has such influence over the patient could intimidate him by his very presence.[11]

## 8. Tribunal decisions

The main function of the Tribunal is to decide whether the patient should be detained in hospital any longer. Under section 72(l)(b) of the Mental Health Act 1983 an unrestricted court order patient must be discharged, if he is not suffering from mental illness, psychopathic disorder, severe mental impairment or mental impairment; or if his disorder is not of a nature or degree which makes it appropriate for him to be liable to be detained in hospital for treatment, or if it is not necessary for the health or safety of the patient or for the protection of other persons that he should be detained and receive such treatment.

Under section 72(3) of the Mental Health Act 1983, unlike the position under the Mental Health Act 1959, the Tribunal can now direct the patient's discharge on a future specified date, rather than straight away on the termination of the hearing. As seen from the above cases[12] this does not mean that the Tribunal can reconsider its decisions on the future date specified.

The criteria for discharging restricted patients, under section 73 of the 1983 Act, are similar to those applicable to unrestricted patients. If the detention in hospital is not appropriate because for instance, the patient is not suffering from mental illness, then the patient must be discharged. Unlike the Home Secretary, the Tribunal has no power to lift the restrictions while leaving the patient to be detained in hospital as an ordinary hospital order patient.

In *R. v. Mental Health Review Tribunal Ex p. Kay*[13] the Merseyside Mental Health Review Tribunal decided to discharge James Kay conditionally. On a judicial review of the decision it was held by the Divisional Court that when a patient who was the subject of a restriction order was found by a Tribunal not to be suffering from mental illness, he remained a "patient" under the Mental Health Act 1983 for the purposes of section 73(2) of that Act and could therefore be conditionally discharged so that he remained liable to recall to hospital. The word "context" at the beginning of section 145(1) permitted the word "patient" to have a different meaning in the group of sections concerned.

If the patient has been transferred from prison under section 47 or 48 of the Mental Health Act 1983, together with a restriction direction under section 49 of that Act, the Tribunal has to decide whether he should be detained in hospital. If they decide that he should not be so detained, then it is up to the Home Secretary to decide whether to transfer him back to prison.

The Tribunal may reach a majority decision and when it is equally divided the presiding member has a casting vote. It must always record its reasons in writing and where it is satisfied that the grounds for a mandatory discharge have been made out, it must, under rule 23 of the 1983 Rules, explain its reasons for its decision.

The decision of the Tribunal must be communicated to the applicant, the patient, the responsible authority, the Home Secretary where the patient is restricted, and to any one else that the Tribunal directs should be informed. This must be done within seven days of the decision in all cases, except that in assessment cases it must be done within three days.

The Tribunal's decision can be challenged either by way of a judicial review under Order 53 of the Rules of the Supreme Court or by asking the Tribunal to state a case for the determination of the High Court on any point of law. Neither of these ways gives a right of appeal on the merits of the case. As decided in *Ex p. Waldron*[14] section 139(1) of the 1983 Act applies only to civil proceedings and does not cover judicial reviews so that such proceedings can be brought even where no negligence or bad faith is alleged.

In *R. v. Mental Health Review Tribunal, ex parte Clatworthy*[15] it was held, on a judicial review, that the reasons given by the Tribunal for refusing to direct the discharge of the applicant from detention in hospital did not show why the case advanced in detail on his behalf had not been accepted. Accordingly as the Tribunal's reasons for their decision were wholly inadequate, the Tribunal's decision was quashed. This followed the decision in *Bone v. Mental Health Review Tribunal*[16] which held that where the Tribunal refuses to direct the discharge of a patient detained under the 1983 Act it must give proper and adequate reasons for its decision, so that the patient will be enabled to know whether the Tribunal has made any error of law in reaching its decision.

## 9. Powers of Tribunals

In *Grant v. Mental Health Review Tribunal*[17] Melvyn Roy Grant was a restricted patient whose case fell under section 73 of the Mental Health Act 1983. The Mental Health Review Tribunal indicated that it would recommend his transfer from one hospital to another if it considered it had the power to do so. Section 72, which did not apply to restricted patients, did confer the power to recommend the transfer of a patient from one hospital to another.

The question for the opinion of the High Court was whether when a Mental Health Review Tribunal was considering an application made under section 70 of the 1983 Act by a patient detained under sections 37 and 41 of the Act, it had the power to make a statutory recommendation for transfer under section 72(3)(a) to another hospital, and by virtue of section 72(3)(b), to further consider his case in the event of any such recommendation not being complied with.

The Court held that section 72(3) authorised a Tribunal to "direct the discharge of a patient on a future date." It was where they did not do that (and ex hypothesi declined to direct that the patient be discharged), that they might "(a) with a view to facilitating his discharge on a future date recommend that he be granted leave of absence or transferred to another hospital or into guardianship and (b) further consider his case in the event of any such recommendation not being complied with."

It was observed by the Court that, save in so far as section 72(3) itself included a limited form of conditional discharge, there was no provision for conditional discharge under section 72 as there was expressly in section 73, where the distinction was drawn between "absolute" and "conditional" discharge. And there was no provision in section 73 echoing or similar to section 72(3).

In the court's view, that plainly indicated the intention of Parliament to repose wider powers on a Tribunal dealing with an unrestricted patient and to limit the power of a Tribunal in directing the conditional discharge of a restricted patient, by enacting specific powers for the Secretary of State to "supervise" such a patient who was conditionally discharged: see section 73(4) and (5) of the 1983 Act.

Section 72(1) of the 1983 Act was not incorporated in section 73: it was only where section 72(1)(b)(i) or (ii) were relevant that there was any such incorporation.

The Court rejected the argument put forward by counsel for the applicant that rule 25 of the Mental Health Review Tribunal Rules was of weight in the construction of the Act itself, and said that a statutory instrument could not confer a jurisdiction not given in the governing statute. The Court went on to find that rule 25 was not ultra vires, but its effect was limited in the circumstances in which the statute empowered recommendation and to an extent therefore it was procedural.

In *Home Secretary v. Mental Health Review Tribunal for Mersey Regional Health Authority*[18] it was held that the word "discharge" in sections 72 to 75 of the 1983 Act meant release from hospital. The Tribunal could not therefore require the patient to remain in hospital if the conditions in section 73(2) applied. Further the deferment of a direction for the conditional discharge of the patient was only permissible where arrangements were to be made for the patient to live in the community. The Tribunal could not defer the direction in order that arrangements could be made for the patient's transfer to another hospital where his detention would be continued.

Two other cases clarifying the position of Tribunals were *R. v. Mental Health Review Tribunal ex P. the Home Department*[19] which decided that where a patient, detained under sections 37 and 41 of the 1983 Act, applies for discharge, a Tribunal has no power to adjourn the proceedings in order to monitor the patient's further progress. *Pickering v. Liverpool Daily Post and Echo Newspapers*[20] overruling *Attorney General v. Associated Newspapers*[21] held that a Tribunal was a court of law for the purposes of the Contempt of Court Act 1981. Under the Mental Health Act 1983 the review tribunals were given the power and duty of applying statutory criteria and on the basis of their findings ordering or refusing to order the release of restricted patients from detention to which they had been subjected by order of bodies which were undoubtedly courts. Furthermore the Tribunals had the power to summon witnesses by subpoena.

## 10. Problems with Mental Health Review Tribunals

A major problem concerns the premature release of patients who have committed offences of violence. Ministers believe that some patients are being released while they are still a danger to the public. Consequently the Home Office and the Department of Health and Social Security published on 21st August 1986 a consultation paper: "Offenders Suffering from Psychopathic Disorder." One of its proposals was to amend section 37 of the Mental Health Act 1983 by removing psychopathic disorder from its scope or enabling judges to impose a minimum period which the offender should spend in hospital, or after treatment, in prison.

*James Kay*,[22] for example, who had been a patient for 14 years at Special Hospitals, after he had raped a girl of 12, was released in April 1986 by a Tribunal, despite pleas from the Home Office Ministers that he was still a potential danger to the public and should not therefore be released. Shortly after his release he was found guilty of two violent attacks on young women and had to be imprisoned for six years.

Another example is *Pickering*,[23] who was sent to Park Lane Hospital after the rape and murder of a girl of 14 in 1972. There is public concern that he too might be released prematurely. When he applied to a Tribunal in March 1986, the Home Office view was that Pickering should not be released as he was still a danger to the public. Subsequently the Tribunal turned down his application despite the views of six psychiatrists that he no longer had a mental disorder.

However, the Tribunal's decision was quashed on a judicial review application as the reasons it gave for its decisions were inadequate. Rule 23(2) of the 1983 Rules provides that the decision by which the Tribunal determines the application should be recorded in writing; the record should be signed by the president and give the reasons for the decision. In particular, where the Tribunal relied on any of the matters set out in section 72(1) or (4) or section 73(1) or (2) of the 1983 Act, it should state its reasons for being satisfied as to the matters mentioned in those sections.

Obviously if such offenders had been sent to prison they would have had to serve long prison sentences even with remission. But as the law stands, the Tribunal is obliged to release any such offender in hospital, if they are satisfied as to the matters set out in section 72(1)(b)(i) or (ii) of the 1983 Act. If, for example, the applicant was not then suffering from mental illness.

Another complication arose in *R. v. Egdell*[24] where the patient's own psychiatrist sent a report to the hospital where he was detained under hospital and restriction orders. It was held that such disclosure could be made in the public interest and copies could be sent to the Home Office and the Tribunal as well.

Although the Government had an opportunity to put matters right by amending section 37 of the Mental Health Act 1983, they have declined to do so.[25]

## 11. Suggested improvements

There is no doubt that in order to avoid the sort of problems illustrated by the above cases, the Tribunal's powers need to be more flexible. Under section 72(1)(b)(i), as read with section 73(1)(a), of the 1983 Act, the Tribunal is obliged to direct the discharge of a hospital order patient, with or without restrictions, if it is satisfied that he is not any longer suffering from mental illness, psychopathic disorder, severe mental impairment or mental impairment or from any of those forms of disorder of a nature or degree which makes it appropriate for him to be liable to be detained in hospital for medical treatment or if they are satisfied that it is not necessary for the health or safety of the patient or for the protection of other persons that he should receive such treatment.

In the case of a restricted patient under section 73(1)(b) of the 1983 Act, the Tribunal additionally has to be satisfied that it is not appropriate for the patient to remain liable to be recalled to hospital for further treatment.

It is quite possible that committing the offence itself, can to a certain extent, relieve the patient's feelings and have a therapeutic effect on him. Added to this, once the patient has been removed from the pressures involved in coping with life, such as family and money problems, and into the calm atmosphere of a hospital and prescribed tranquillising medicine, the symptoms of his mental disorder can diminish or disappear completely.

Consequently, psychiatrists are liable to say that he has been cured. But when the Tribunal discharges him back into the environment where he faces the problems and pressures which caused his illness in the first place, and where again he is subjected to temptation and the taking of his medicine is no longer supervised, his symptoms are liable to reappear.

In order to contain this problem of patients being released and then offending again, it would assist the situation if the Tribunals had more powers. Such as, in the case of a restricted patient removing the restrictions and detaining him as an ordinary hospital order patient. Or if Tribunals had the power to transfer a restricted patient to another hospital, to ensure that his progress was monitored or transfer him to prison if he no longer suffered from mental illness but nevertheless was still considered to be dangerous.

It is not logical to empower Tribunals to absolutely discharge restricted patients and yet to deny the same Tribunals, at least, the power, similar to that in section 72(3)(a) of the 1983 Act in relation to unrestricted patients, to transfer restricted patients from one hospital to another or into guardianship, with a view to facilitating their discharge by allowing them to adapt themselves for it in easy stages.

## CHAPTER 9: CONCLUSION

### 1. Reform of the defence of insanity

As can be seen from what is said in chapter 2, the defence of insanity is now virtually unusable. In any future reform of the mental health legislation, top priority must be, therefore, its replacement by a workable insanity defence. Our judges are still firmly wedded to the McNaghten Rules, as shown by Lord Diplock's remarks in *R. v. Sullivan*[1] in referring to the fact that the nomenclature adopted by the medical profession may change from time to time but the meaning of "disease of mind" as the cause of "a defect of reason" remained unchanged for the purposes of applying the McNaghten Rules. Thus, as Lord Diplock said in *Sullivan*[2] it does not lie within the power of the courts to alter the test of insanity. Only Parliament could do that.

It is a great pity that the golden opportunity presented by the Mental Health (Amendment) Act 1982 was missed. That Act introduced several reforms relating to mental illness, proposed by the Butler Committee, such as remands to hospital for a medical report or for treatment and for interim hospital orders. However, a further proposal relating to the defence of insanity in Chapter 18 of the same Butler Report was not tackled in that Act. It is possible that as the 1982 Act was primarily concerned with civil matters and not with substantive criminal defences, the insanity proposals will be dealt with in a suitable Bill in future. The fact that a further opportunity was missed in the Criminal Procedure (Insanity and Unfitness to Plead) Act 1991 does not bode well for any useful reform of the insanity defence in the near future.

Briefly, the Butler Committee proposed that the word "insanity" and the McNaghten Rules be replaced by a verdict of "not guilty on evidence of mental disorder." The verdict would apply where the magistrates or the jury find that the prosecution have failed to prove the offence because of the lack of "mens rea" due to evidence of the defendant's mental disorder. Or, where the prosecution have proved the offence but there is evidence that the defendant was at the time suffering from "severe mental illness," or "severe mental subnormality" (see paragraph 18.30 of the Report). "Severe mental illness" is still not defined in current legislation but the Butler Committee suggested a definition in paragraph 18.35 of their Report (see section 3 of this Chapter). "Severe subnormality" was defined in section 4 of the 1959 Act and has now been replaced by "severe mental impairment" in section 1 of the 1983 Act.

Where there is an acquittal due to the failure of the prosecution to prove the offence due to lack of "mens rea" or where the offence has been made out but it is proved that the defendant was at the time suffering from severe mental illness or severe mental impairment and he is, therefore, held not to be liable for the offence, the court would have wide powers. As in fact now provided for in Criminal Procedure (Insanity and Unfitness to Plead) Act 1991. Such as the making of a hospital order, with or without restrictions.[3]

As has been pointed out already,[4] the imbalance in the present system, under section 37 of the Mental Health Act 1983 is that whereas the Regional Health Authorities or the Secretary of State are not obliged to carry out their responsibilities in providing hospital places, the prison service is obliged to provide prison places where a hospital order can not be made. This militates against the making of a hospital order and in favour of a prison sentence. However, if the Butler Committee's recommendations were followed, the alternative of prison sentence would be removed for those found "not guilty on evidence of mental disorder;'' the defendant would have to be discharged, made subject to a non-penal order or found a place in hospital.

It is interesting to note that at present where prison is not an alternative, as with the special verdict, the Home Secretary is given two months during which to find a hospital place. He invariably does so.[5] If the Butler Report proposals, relating to the defence of insanity were fully implemented, pleas of insanity would not be limited to 2 or 3 a year at the most, as now happens, but would be considerably increased, probably to include all those who plead diminished responsibility now, as well as many offenders who now come under section 37 of the Mental Health Act 1983.

However, the main drawback with the Butler recommendation on insanity is that, as the Report itself states at paragraphs 18.36 and 18.37, it would be possible for the severe mental disorder to have no link with the offence. Paragraph 18.36 of the Report states that "the mental conditions included in our definitions are of such severity that the causative links between the offence and the defendant's mental condition can safely be presumed." The presence of such presumption is repeated at the end of paragraph 18.37 and it further states "that the inquiry to establish that it existed would be too difficult to make."

Surely for the Butler proposal to be justifiable to the public, as the Report admits in paragraph 18.36 it would have to be, it would be necessary to establish a causative link, which would not always be as difficult as the Butler Report suggests. Why should someone with delusions about his abilities as a tennis player be found not guilty of murdering his father solely for the purpose of inheriting his money? The delusion has nothing to do with the offence. Even if he killed the champion tennis player under the delusion that he would then become the champion, a verdict of not guilty on evidence of mental disorder would still not be justifiable to the public.

It would be justifiable only if the delusion, if true, would have excused the killing; if, for instance, the delusion was that someone was about to run him over and the only way he could save his life was to kill the driver. This would admittedly take us some way back towards the McNaghten Rules. That is, he did not know the nature or quality of the act he was doing; but without some such causative link the Butler recommendation would not be justifiable. This could be the reason why it has not been possible to implement this part of the Butler Report.

The Law Commission[6] recognised this weakness in the Butler proposal but they felt bound to draft the Criminal Code to give effect to it. However, they suggest a compromise, which they say could easily be provided in the Code. Their suggestion is that the presumption of a causative link between the offence and the defendant's mental condition should be rebuttable. That is, the prosecution would be free to prove that the defendant's mental condition had nothing to do with his offence. It remains to be seen whether this compromise is politically acceptable or whether positive proof of a causative link would be demanded before the defence was made available.

The way forward would be to implement the Butler proposals with the requirement of proof of a causal link. If this were not acceptable, it would be possible as a first step, to make the link between the offence and the defendant's mental condition a rebuttable presumption. If this led to difficulties because it was felt that too many defendants were being acquitted on evidence of mental disorder where the mental disorder was not connected with the offence, the provisions could be further tightened up. It is interesting to note in this connection that so far as hospital orders are concerned, there does not have to be any connection between the offence and the mental disorder.[7]

It would be better to reform the insanity defence along the lines suggested and to fine tune it at a later stage, if necessary, rather than keeping the McNaghten Rules which are clearly not working and the diminished responsibility defence which works, but has unsatisfactory aspects in allowing, or almost requiring, psychiatrists to give evidence outside the limits of their own science. (See section 7 of this chapter).

## 2. The meaning of mental illness

In order for the mental health legislation to operate satisfactorily there is a desperate need for an adequate definition of mental illness. The Butler Report[8] has recommended a definition of severe mental illness and Lord Denning has lamented the lack of such a definition in *W. v. L.*[9] but in spite of these criticisms, the opportunity to make provision for a definition was missed when the Mental Health Act 1959 was amended in 1982 and consolidated in the Mental Health Act 1983.

The proposed definition recommended in the Butler Report is analysed in the following section of this chapter. In *W. v. L.*, Lord Denning drew attention[10] to the fact that "psychopathic disorder" was a ground for compulsory detention under section 26(2)(a)(ii) of the 1959 Act[11] only if the patient was under twenty-one. Since the husband was twenty-three at the time, then under section 26(2)(a)(i) of the 1959 Act in order to be compulsorily detained he had to be suffering from "mental illness.'' His Lordship continued: "But strangely enough, 'mental illness' is not defined. It defines everything else, but it does not define 'mental illness.' It is presumably something worse than 'psychopathic disorder' since it applies to patients of any age. But what is it? It is apparent that this problem - which is a mixed legal and medical problem - perplexed all those concerned in this case. A clinical meeting of experts was held on February 5, 1973. No one had any doubt that the husband was suffering from 'psychopathic disorder', but several doubted whether he could be classed as 'mentally ill'... If the matter stopped there, there would be no lawful means of detaining the husband without the wife's consent. But on February 13th, 1973, Dr. Acton-Stephens, a distinguished consultant, came to the conclusion that the husband was suffering from mental illness of a nature and degree which would warrant his detention in hospital."

In the absence of any definition, it is a well known canon of construction of statutes that where a term is used in an Act of Parliament, which affects everyone generally, the term has the meaning attached to it in the common and ordinary use of language.[12] As pointed out by Lawton L.J. in *W. v. L.*[13] the term mental illness should have its natural meaning and not any meaning which the two medical practitioners give it in the context of what they consider to be the mental health norm. It should be for the jury to decide whether the accused is mentally ill or not on the basis of the judge's directions, which would of course take into account the evidence of the medical practitioners.

## 3. Proposed definition of "severe mental illness"

As stated above, although the Butler Committee proposed a definition of "mental illness" and Lord Denning has criticised the lack of definition in *W. v. L.*[14] there is still no definition in the Mental Health Act 1983. This leads to enormous difficulties. It is left to psychiatrists to say what is mental illness with no legislative guidance whatever. This gives them a very wide discretion.

Thus another beneficial effect of the implementation of the Butler Committee's proposals relating to a verdict of "not guilty on evidence of mental disorder" would be that the psychiatrists' difficult decision in deciding the form of mental disorder under section 1(2) of the 1983 Act would be facilitated. The Butler Report[15] proposed the following definition for "severe mental illness:"

> "A mental illness is severe when it has one or more of the following characteristics:-
>
> (a) Lasting impairment of intellectual functions shown by failure of memory, orientation, comprehension and learning capacity.
>
> (b) Lasting alteration of mood of such degree as to give rise to delusional appraisal of the patient's situation, his past or his future, or that of others, or to lack of any appraisal.
>
> (c) Delusional beliefs, persecutory, jealous or grandiose.
>
> (d) Abnormal perceptions associated with delusional misinterpretation of events.
>
> (e) Thinking so disordered as to prevent reasonable appraisal of the patient's situation or reasonable communication with others."

It would need to be considered whether the change made by the

1982 Act of the term "severe subnormality" used in the 1959 Act, which was the context of Lord Butler's formulation, to "severe mental impairment," now in section 1(2) of the 1983 Act, necessitates any modification to the proposed Butler formulation of the insanity defence.

The 1983 Act definitions have added an element of "abnormally aggressive or seriously irresponsible conduct." On balance, this additional element would need to be excluded from the Butler Committee's formulation of the defence of insanity. At the time of the Butler Report, section 4 of the 1959 Act defined "severe subnormality" by reference to the incapacity of the patient to live "an independent life or of guarding himself against serious exploitation." While it made sense to recommend that if someone was not capable of living an independent life or guarding against serious exploitation he should not be held to be criminally responsible, it is not quite so satisfactory to suggest, in the terms of the current definition, that someone whose incomplete development of mind is associated with "abnormally aggressive or seriously irresponsible conduct" should also be exempt from criminal responsibility.

Thus to make sense of the Butler Report's recommendation it would be preferable to revert to the terminology of the 1959 Act definitions for this purpose. While the test of the patient's inability to live an independent life or guard against serious exploitation has disappeared from the definitions in the 1983 Act, it is still a valid test in section 72(2)(b) of the 1983 Act, where a Mental Health Review Tribunal has to have regard to it before determining whether certain patients should be discharged from hospital.

A further matter which will need to be considered is the lack of link, in the Butler Report proposals, between the mental disorder and the offence. (See section 1 of this Chapter). Surely the proposed Butler Report defence of insanity should succeed only where a causative link between the offence and the mental disorder was established. Or, as a first step, the link could be a rebuttable presumption.

If the above definition were to be adopted, modified in the ways suggested above, it would mean that psychiatrists would give their evidence on legally established criteria. Thus their task would be eased and their power limited. The scope of the defence would also be limited. It is interesting to note that a few years after the Butler Report, the Royal College of Psychiatrists found that the proposed definition (without the abnormally aggressive or seriously irresponsible conduct element) was broadly acceptable.[16]

### 4. Diminished responsibility

If a sensible insanity defence were to be available, possibly along the lines indicated in the previous section, there would not be any need for a diminished responsibility defence under section 2 of the Homicide Act 1957. That defence was introduced when certain types of murder were still capital offences, in order to introduce some flexibility into the system of sentencing for an unlawful killing. When murder ceased to be a capital offence, it continued to carry a mandatory life sentence, which meant that some flexibility was still needed; notably to allow the hospitalisation of those who suffered from mental disorder. Especially in view of the virtual collapse of the insanity defence due to the inflexibility of the McNaghten Rules and until the enactment of the Criminal Procedure (Insanity and Unfitness to Plead) Act 1991, the sentence following a special verdict of "not guilty by reason of insanity."

If the insanity defence were not limited to the McNaghten Rules, that is to whether the offender knew what he was doing or whether he knew that it was wrong, but extended to cover a person suffering from severe mental illness or severe mental impairment, then, on balance, the defence of diminished responsibility would not be needed and would, in any case, probably fall into disuse.

### 5. Hospital orders

However, if "severe mental illness" were defined for the purposes of the defence of insanity, there would still be cases of mentally disordered offenders, who while they were outside the definition of "severe mental illness" and "severe mental impairment," still needed treatment in hospital rather than punishment in prison. Assuming that the defence of insanity were to be reformed and limited to the major disorders along the lines of the Butler Committee's recommendations[17] there would still be those suffering from mental illness, psychopathic disorder or mental impairment, mentioned in section 1(2) of the Mental Health Act 1983, who would need the protection of section 37 of that Act.

### 6. The role of psychiatrists

In *R. v. Turner*[18] Lawton L.J. restated the well known principle that "the opinion of scientific men upon proven facts may be given by men of science within their own science. An expert's opinion is admissible to furnish the court with scientific information which is likely to be outside the experience and knowledge of the judge or jury."

Psychiatrists are undoubtedly men of science but the difficulty is in deciding when they are testifying within their own science and when they are going beyond the proper confines of their science. The main problem is that in psychiatry it is difficult to draw a line between matters of fact and matters of value. An expert can give his opinion on matters of fact; but matters of value, which may involve decisions on principle or policy, are not within the proper confines of a psychiatrist's science. Unless this line is carefully drawn psychiatrists can easily usurp the functions of others in the legal system.[19]

If they testify to the naked conclusion, for instance, instead of providing information about the accused to assist the jury in making the ultimate judgement about guilt or innocence, they would be usurping the functions of the jury. If they give their own meaning to statutory terms, such as "responsibility" in section 2 of the Homicide Act 1957, as they often do, they are usurping the functions of the judge. Where they testify on the basis of convictions of general policy, for example, that persons who may be mentally ill in some way should not be sent to prison, they usurp the functions of Parliament.

Particularly in diminished responsibility cases where there is no dispute about the acts or omissions of the accused, the psychiatrist is asked to testify, in effect, whether in his opinion the accused should be convicted. That is of course the function of the jury. Further, in such cases the psychiatrist can hardly help giving his opinion on the question whether persons suffering from mental illness of a certain kind should be punished; but that is surely a matter for Parliament. It is no fault of the psychiatrists that they are pushed into this unenviable position. It is the system which needs reforming. All that the psychiatrist does is to assist the court to the best of his ability in any way that he is asked to do.

It would seem that since *R. v. Byrne*[20] it has been established that inability to exercise will power to control physical acts due to abnormality of mind is sufficient to entitle the accused to the defence of diminished responsibility. It is thus open to psychiatrists to say that the accused acted on an irresistible impulse.

The present position is certainly not satisfactory. If Parliament implemented the Butler recommendation,[21] that if the jury believes that the accused, at the time of his alleged offence was suffering from severe mental illness or severe subnormality, it should return a verdict of "not guilty on evidence of mental disorder," the role of the psychiatrist would be limited to saying, whether at the time of the act, the accused was or was not suffering from mental disorder, as defined. This would be within the psychiatrist's competence and he would not be usurping anyone else's functions. However, the difficulties mentioned in section 1 of this Chapter would need to be overcome before the Butler recommendations on the defence of insanity could be implemented.

## 7. Law Commission proposals

Clauses 35 and 36 of the Draft Code proposed by the Law Commission[22] substitute for the McNaghten Rules a verdict of "not guilty by reason of mental disorder," as proposed in Chapter 18 of the Butler Report. They provide that such a verdict should be returned either, under Clause 35(1), when the defendant committed the offence charged but was at the time suffering from severe mental disorder; or under Clause 36, when the evidence of the defendant's mental disorder at the time of his act or omission is the reason why he is not proved to have committed the offence charged. In each case the mental disorder has to be proved on the balance of probabilities by either the prosecution or the defendant.

Clause 34 of the Draft Criminal Code defines mental disorder, not by reference to the definition in section 1(2) of the Mental Health Act 1983, as the Butler Committee would have done, but far more narrowly. It confines the definition to severe mental illness and severe mental handicap. Clause 39 of the Draft Criminal Code provides for a Schedule of provisions concerning disposal of persons found not guilty on evidence of mental disorder.

However, nothing has been done about the implementation of the Law Commission's proposals in spite of the opportunity presented by the enactment of the Criminal Procedure (Insanity and Unfitness to Plead) Act 1991.

# NOTES

## CHAPTER: 1

1.  Kenny (1962) Outlines of Criminal Law 18th Edition (Cambridge), paragraph 54.

2.  Hale (1736) The History of the Pleas of the Crown Vol. 1 (Savoy) pp.31-32 where it is stated: "if they are totally deprived of the use of reason, they cannot be guilty of capital offences ... "

3.  Walker N. (1973) Crime and Insanity in England Vol. 1 (Edinburgh University Press) p.66.

4.  Ibid. p.66.

5.  (1729) Old Bailey Sessions Papers Vol. 1 Second Sessions p.11.

6.  (1730) Old Bailey Sessions Papers Vol. 1 Third Sessions p.16.

7.  (1730) Old Bailey Sessions Papers Vol. 1 Third Sessions p.13.

8.  *R. v. Peter Bluck* (1730) Old Bailey Sessions Papers Vol. 1 Sixth Sessions p. 12.

9.  *R. v. Roger Bow* (1733) Old Bailey Sessions Papers Vol. 5 p.133.

10. (1724) 16 St. Tr. 695 at 765.

11. (1800) 27 St. Tr. 1281.

12. (1738) Old Bailey Sessions Papers, Vol. 10 p. 108.

13. (1843) 10 Cl. & Fin. 200.

14. (1843) 10 Cl. & Fin. 200 at 210.

**CHAPTER: 1 cont.**

15.  (1849) 4 Cox C.C. 57.

16.  Griew E, The Future of Diminished Responsibility (1988) Crim.L.R. 75 at 78 and Kenny A, The Expert in Court (1983) L.Q.R. Vol. 99 p.197.

17.  [1984] A.C. 156.

18.  (1849) 4 Cox C.C. 149.

19.  (1868) 11 Cox C.C. 341.

20.  Report of the Royal Commission on Capital Punishment Cmnd. 8932 (1953).

21.  Walker N. McCabe S. Crime and Insanity in England Vol. 2 (1972) p. 59.

22.  Now section 40 of the National Health Service Act 1973.

23.  The law relating to the possibility of instituting proceedings against a Minister of the Crown for breach of statutory duty is developing fast. See *Bourgoin* [1985] 3 All E.R. 585 and *Herbage* [1986] 3 W.L.R. 504.

24.  Report of the Committee on Mentally Abnormal Offenders. (1975) Cmnd. 6244. ("Butler Report"). Paragraph 3.40.

25.  Butler Report op. cit. paragraph 3.42.

26.  Butler Report op. cit. paragraph 3.43.

**CHAPTER: 2**

1.  Royal Commission on Capital Punishment. (1953) Cmnd.8932. Paragraph 278.

2.  *R. v. Layton* (1849) 4 Cox 149; and *R v. Smith* (1910) 6 Crim. App. R. 19.

**CHAPTER: 2 cont.**

3.      [1935] A.C. 462.

4.      *R. v. Judith Defour* (1733) Old Bailey Sessions Papers Vol. 5
        p. 82 and *R. v. Dix* (1982) 74 Cr. App. R. 306.

5.      27 St. Tr. 1281.

6.      27 St. Tr. 1281 at 1354.

7.      For present position see section 1 of the Criminal Procedure
        (Insanity) Act 1964.

8.      Now section 4 of the 1964 Act, as substituted by section 2
        of the Criminal Procedure (Insanity and Unfitness to Plead)
        Act 1991.

9.      (1843) 10 Cl. & Fin. 200.

10.     (1843) 10 Cl. & Fin. 200.

11.     Butler Report op. cit.

12.     Dell. S. Wanted: An Insanity Defence that Can be Used.
        [1983] Crim. L.R. 431.

13.     (1843) 10 Cl. & Fin. 200.

14.     Royal Commission on Capital Punishment. (1953)
        Cmnd. 8932. Paragraph 278.

15.     (1960) 44 Cr. App. R. 246.

16.     [1984] A.C. 156.

17.     [1991] 2 All E.R. 769.

18.     [1983] 2 All E.R. 503.

19.     [1973] Q.B. 910.

**CHAPTER: 2  cont.**

20. [1983] 2 All E.R. 503 at 507.

21. [1982] A.C. 341.

22. [1982] A.C. 341 at 356.

23. [1957] 2 Q.B. 396.

24. [1983] Crim. L.R. 681.

25. 3 All E.R. 848.

26. [1984] A.C. 156 at 172.

27. *R v. Burgess*

28. [1957] 1 Q.B. 399.

29. [1970] 1 All E.R. 642.

30. [1968] 3 All E.R. 557.

**CHAPTER: 3**

1. Walker N, (1973) Op. Cit. pp.142-5.

2. (1958) 42 Cr. App. R. 145.

3. (1979) 69 Cr. App. R. 104.

4. (1976) Unreported but cited in *R. v. Vinagre* (1979) 69 Cr. App. R. 104.

5. (1968) 52 Cr. App. R. 130.

6. (1962) 46 Cr. App. R. 269.

7. (1977) 66 Cr. App. R. 25.

**CHAPTER: 3 cont.**

**8.**   (1987) 84 Cr. App. R. 255.

**9.**   (1982) 74 Cr. App. R. 30.

**10.**   Dell S. Diminished Responsibility Reconsidered [1982] Crim. L.R. 809. ("Dell Diminished Responsibility").

**11.**   [1988] Crim. L.R. 241.

**12.**   Wooton B. Diminished Responsibility. A Layman's View. (1960) 76 L.Q.R. 224.

**13.**   Dell Diminished Responsibility op. cit. pp.812,817.

**14.**   Dell Diminished Responsibility op. cit. p. 817.

**15.**   Criminal Law Revision Committee. Fourteenth Report (1980) Offences Against the Person Cmnd. 7844, paragraphs 92-94.

**16.**   Report of the Committee on Mentally Abnormal Offenders (1975) Cmnd. 6244. ("Butler Report") paragraph 19.16.

**17.**   Butler Report op. cit. paragraph 18.4.

**18.**   See now Section 5 of, and Schedule 1, to the Criminal Procedure (Insanity Act) 1964, as substituted by the Criminal Procedure (Insanity and Unfitness to Plead) Act 1991.

**19.**   Dell S. Murder into Manslaughter (1984) p. 31, note. ("Dell Murder").

**20.**   (1960) 44 Cr. App. R. 246.

**21.**   Dell Murder op. cit. pp.36-37 and Butler Report paragraph 19.20.

**22.**   *R. v. Duca* (1959) 43 Cr. App. R. 167.

**23.**   Dell Murder op. cit. p. 38.

**CHAPTER: 3 cont.**

**24.** *R. v. Tandy* [19881 Crim.L.R. 308.

**25.** Dell Murder op. cit. p.52.

**26.** [1961] 2 Q.B. 237.

**27.** Butler Report op. cit. paragraphs 18.6 and 18.35.

**28.** Butler Report op. cit. paragraph 4.39.

**29.** Dell Murder op. cit. p.54.

**30.** Butler Report op. cit. paragraph 19.11(c).

**CHAPTER: 4**

**1.** The Arizona Laws 1977 ch. 142, codified as Arizona Revised Statutes, sections 13-502. 13-701, 13-702.

**2.** The New York Laws 1965 ch. 1030, p. 1542, codified as New York Penal Law section 30.05.

**3.** Law and Mental Health: International Perspectives Volume 1 Ed. David N. Weisstub (1984) p.6. ("Weisstub").

**4.** The Georgia Laws 1968 p. 1270, codified as Georgia Code Annotated, section 702.

**5.** Weisstub op. cit. p. 7.

**6.** Goldstein A.S. The Insanity Defence (1967) p. 71.

**7.** Weisstub op. cit. p. 7.

**8.** Missouri Laws 1977 p. 658, codified as Missouri Annotated Statutes, Article 562.086.

**9.** 22 Cal. 3d 333, 149 Cal. Reptr. 275,583 P.2d 1318 (1978).

**CHAPTER: 4 cont.**

10. 81 Ala.577, 2So.854 (1987).

11. 154 S.W.2d 348,202 Ark. 921 (1941).

12. 60 Wash. 106, 110 P. 1020 (1910).

13. 392 U.S. 514 (1968).

14. Weisstub op. cit. p.12.

15. 60 Cal.2d 482, 35 Cal.Reptr. 77, 386 P.2d 677 (1963).

16. 61 Cal.2d 795, 40 Cal. Reptr. 271,394 P.2d 959 (1964).

17. 10 Cal.2d 750, 111 Cal.Reptr. 910, 518 P.2d 342 (1974).

18. Weisstub op. cit. p. 14.

19. California laws 1981 ch. 404, codified as California Penal Code, section 28.

20. Weisstub op. cit. p. 15.

21. 653 P.2d 385 (Colo.1982).

22. Keedy E.R. Insanity and Criminal Responsibility. Harvard Law Review, 1917,30, 535-560,724-738 at p. 536.

23. Montana Laws 1977 ch. 196 section 3 repealed the provisions relating to insanity and diminished capacity, thus leaving only the statutory provision authorising consideration of mental disorder in determining whether "mens rea" had been proved. Codified as Montana Revised Codes Annotated, sections 46-14 -101, 46-14 -102.

24. Weisstub op. cit. p.18.

25. Hale op. cit. p.42.

120

**CHAPTER: 4 cont.**

26. Weisstub op. cit. p. 19.

27. *Furman v. Georgia* 408 U.S. 238 (1972).

28. 428 U.S. 153 (1976).

29. Weisstub op. cit. p.20.

30. Ibid p.22.

31. Ibid. p. 22.

32. Smith G.A. & Hall J.A. Evaluating Michigan's guilty but mentally ill verdict: An empirical study. University of Michigan Journal of Law Reform, 1982, 161(1), 77-114.

33. Ibid. pp. 104-5.

34. 440 N.E.rd 1109 (Ind. 1982).

35. Criss M.L. & Racine D.R. Impact of change in legal standard of those adjudicated not guilty by reason of insanity 1975-79. Bulletin of American Academy of Psychiatry and the Law, 1980 8(3), 261-271.

36. 160 U.S. 469 (1985).

37. 343 U.S. 790 (1952).

38. 397 U.S. 358 (1970).

39. Weisstub op. cit. p. 24.

40. Weihofen H. Mental disorder as a criminal defence. Buffalo: Dennis & Co., Inc., 1954 p. 362.

41. 406 U.S. 715 (1972).

42. *Benham v. Edwards* 678 F2d 511 (5th Cir. 1982).

**CHAPTER: 4 cont.**

43. Weisstub op. cit. p. 25.

44. Ibid. p. 25.

45. 222 F. 2d 398 (D.C.Cir. 1954).

46. 254 F. 2d 725 (D.C.Cir. 1957).

47. 591 P. 2d 1031 (Colo. 1979).

48. 273 S.E.2d 87 (W.Va. 1980).

49. 611 S.W.2d 745 (Ark. 1981).

50. 214 F. 2d 862 (D.C.Cir. 1954).

51. 417 F. 2d 969 (D.C.Cir. 1972).

52. Butler Report op. cit. paragraph 18.17.

53. Butler Report op. cit. paragraph 18.36.

54. 525 F.Supp 1342 (D.C. 1981).

55. Weisstub op. cit. p. 28.

56. Ibid. p. 34.

57. Alaska Laws 1982, ch.143 section 27, codified as Alaska Statutes, sections 12.47.010(a), 12.47.030.

58. Delaware Laws Vol. 63, ch. 328, 1982, codified as Delaware Code Annotated, Title 11, section 401, 408.

59. Weisstub op. cit. p.30.

60. For example Alaska, Delaware, and Texas.

61. For example Alaska. See Note 57.

**CHAPTER: 4  cont.**

**62.**   Weisstub op. cit. p. 31.

**63.**   103 U.S. 3943 (1983) p. 3052.

**64.**   Weisstub op. cit. p. 33.

**65.**   Hoggett Mental Health Act 1983 op. cit. at p.181.

**66.**   Butler Report op. cit. paragraph 14.7.

**67.**   Steadman and Morissey, The Insanity Defence (1986) 484
Annals of the American Academy of Political & Social
Science 68.Law Commission Report No. 143 (1985).

**68.**   Law Commission Report  No. 143  (1985)

**69.**   Brooks: The merits of Abolishing the Insanity Defence
(1985) 477 Annals of the American Academy of Political and
Social Science 125, 131.

**70.**   Mich.  Stat.  Ann. paragraphs 28-1059 (1985).

**71.**   Pa. Const. Stat. Ann. tit.  IE3 paragraphs 314(c) and 315(b)

**72.**   18 U.S.C. paragraph 20(a).

**73.**   39 Cal. 3d 765 (1985).

**74.**   Butler Report op. cit. paragraphs 18.42-18.45.

**CHAPTER: 5**

**1.**   (1981) 4 E.H.R.R. 181.

**2.**   Butler Report op. cit.

**3.**   D.H.S.S. Review of the Mental Health Act 1959 (1976).

**4.**   Review of the Mental Health Act 1959 (1978) Cmnd. 7320.

**CHAPTER: 5 cont.**

5.   Reform of the Mental Health Legislation (1981) Cmnd. 8405.

6.   Gostin L, A Human Condition: The Law relating to Mentally
     Abnormal Offenders Vol 2 (1977) Chapter 6.

7.   Butler Report op. cit. Chapter 12.

8.   Hogett B. The Mental Health Act 1983 [1983] P.L. 172 at

9.   (1981) 4 E.H.R.R. 181.

10.  (1979) 2 E.H.R.R. 387.

11.  Gostin L, A Review of the Mental Health (Amendment) Act,
     New Law Journal December 9, 1982, page 1152.

12.  McNair J. in Bolam v. Friern Barnet Hospital Management
     Committee [19571 2 All E.R. 118.

13.  William G.L. (1983) Textbook of Criminal Law 2nd Ed.
     p. 572

14.  [1986] 2 All E.R. 306.

15.  The Times May 25 1989.

16.  [1990] 2 AC 1.

17.  H.C. Debates, Special Standing Committee, Thirteenth
     Sitting (15 June 1982) Col. 511.

18.  Gostin L A Human Condition op. cit. Vol. 1, Part III.

19.  The Mental Health Act Commission Second Biennial Report
     1985-87 (October 1987) H.M.S.O.

20.  Now section 121(2) of the 1983 Act.

21.  The Times May 27, 1988.

**CHAPTER: 6**

1.    [1983] 1 W.L.R. 335.

2.    (1984) 80 Cr. App. R. 366.

3.    [1962] Crim. L.R. 647.

4.    Section 60(3).

5.    Butler Report op. cit. paragraph 14.7.

6.    Butler Report op. cit. paragraph 3.40.

7.    Ibid. paragraph 3.40.

8.    Ibid. paragraph 14.5

9.    Ibid. paragraph 14.4.

10.    Ibid. paragraph 14.2.

11.    Ibid. paragraph 14.3.

12.    Hoggett B. Mental Health Law 2nd Ed. (1984) p. 145.

13.    Butler Report op. cit. paragraph 14.7.

14.    H.C. Debates Special Standing Committee 13th Sitting (June 15th, 1982) Col. 511.

15.    Section 39 was introduced as a compromise at the Report Stage.H.C. Debates Vol. 29 (October 18th, 1982) Cols. 36-40.

16.    The Times June 15, 1983.

17.    [1961] 2 Q.B. 237.

18.    (1968) 52 Cr. App. R. 130.

19.    (1975) 60 Cr. App. R. 320.

**CHAPTER: 6 cont.**

20.   H.C. Debates (22 March 1982) Cols. 697-8.

21.   The Times October 20, 1984.

22.   The Times January 22, 1985.

23.   For example, the New Law Journal June 28, 1985 p.626.

24.   The Times January 22, 1985.

25.   Butler Report op. cit. paragraph 1.3.

26.   The Lancet February 16, 1985 402.

27.   New Law Journal June 28, 1985 p.626.

28.   [1961] 3 All E.R. 616.

29.   (1966) 50 Cr. App. R. 242.

30.   [1971] Crim. L.R. 664.

31.   [1964] Crim. L.R. 236.

32.   The Times January 14, 1988.

33.   The Times November 26, 1987.

34.   [1948] 1 K.B. 223.

35.   H.C. Debates Vol. 123 (26 November 1987) Cols.377-80.

36.   de Smith S.A. Judicial Review of Administrative Action 4th Ed. (1980) p. 528.

37.   Ibid. p. 529.

38.   [1979] 1 W.L.R. 637

**CHAPTER: 6 cont.**

**39.** Ibid. Lord Denning's judgement p. 649.

**40.** Gostin L, Mental Health Services op.cit. paragraph 15.08.

**CHAPTER: 7**

**1.** Butler Report op. cit. paragraph 14.22.

**2.** (1968) 52 Cr. App. R. 514.

**3.** [1967] 1 All E.R. 895.

**4.** Butler Report op. cit. paragraph 7.23.

**5.** Butler Report op. cit. paragraph 7.23.

**6.** Gostin 1, A Human Condition op. cit. Vol 2, p.75.

**7.** The Report of the Royal Commission on the Law Relating to Mental Illness and Mental Deficiency, Cmnd. 169, paragraph 519.

**8.** [1961] 3 All E.R. 616.

**9.** (1981) 73 Cr. App. R. 281.

**10.** (1981) 4 E.H.R.R. 181.

**11.** [1987] 3 All E.R. 8.

**12.** The Times May 11, 1986.

**13.** Home Office, D.H.S.S. Consultation Paper; "Offenders suffering from Pyschopathic Disorder," 21 August 1986.

**14.** House of Lords Hansard 22 January 1987 Col. 1027.

**15.** Gostin L, A Human Condition op. cit. p. 97.

**CHAPTER: 7 cont.**

16. Butler Report op. cit. paragraphs 4.39-4.43.

17. [1967] 1 All E.R. 895.

18. (1974) 58 Cr. App. R. 453.

19. (1966) 50 Cr. App. R. 242.

20. [1967] 1 All E.R. 895.

21. [1976] Crim. L.R. 636.

22. Hoggett B. The Mental Health Act 1983 ("Hoggett") [1983] P.L. 172.

23. (1981) 3 Cr. App. R.(S) 112.

24. (1985) 7 Cr. App. R. *(S)* 310.

25. Hoggett op. cit. p. 182.

26. Hoggett op. cit. p. 182.

27. Gostin L, A Human Condition Vol 2 op. cit. p. 75.

28. [1986] 1 All E.R. 99. For details see Chapter 8.

29. See note 13.

30. Butler Report op. cit. paragraph 14.22.

31. [1973] 3 All E.R. 884.

32. (1979) 2 E.H.R.R. 387.

33. Butler Report op. cit. paragraphs 1.13, 18.35 and App.10.

34. Ashworth and Gostin "Mentally Disordered Offenders and the Sentencing Process." [1984] Crim. L. R. 195.

## CHAPTER: 8

1.     Report of the Royal Commission on the Law Relating to Mental Illness and Mental Deficiency 1954-57 Cmnd. 169.

2.     Application No. 6998/75, (1981) 4 E.H.R.R. 181.

3.     Rule 8(3) of the Mental Health Review Tribunal Rules 1983, S.I. 1983 No. 942 ("The Rules").

4.     Rule 8(2) of the Rules.

5.     The Times June 2, 1986.

6.     [1987] 3 All E.R. 8.

7.     [1987] 3 All E.R. 8 at 11.

8.     [1986] 3 All E.R. 239.

9.     Hoggett B. (1984) Mental Health Law 2nd Ed. p. 266 ("Hoggett").

10.     Hoggett op. cit. p. 267.

11.     Hoggett op. cit. p. 268.

12.     *Secretary of State v. Oxford Regional M.H.R.T.*, note 6 above and *R. v. Yorkshire M.H.R.T.*, note 8 above.

13.     The Times May 25, 1988.

14.     [1985] 3 W.L.R. 1090.

15.     [1985] 3 W.L.R. 699.

16.     [1985] 3 All E.R. 330.

17.     The Times April 26, 1986.

18.     [1986] 3 All E.R. 233.

**CHAPTER: 8  cont.**

**19.**   The Times March 25, 1987.

**20.**   The Times January 18, 1990.

**21.**   [1989] 1 W.L.R. 322.

**22.**   The Times May 11, 1986.

**23.**   [1986] 1 All E.R. 99.

**24.**   The Times December 14, 1988.

**25.**   Hansard (Lords) for 22 January 1987, Col. 1027.

**CHAPTER: 9**

**1.**   [1984] 1 A.C. 156 at 172.

**2.**   [1984] 1 A.C. 156 at 173.

**3.**   Butler Report op. cit. Chapter 12. Now section 35, 36 and 38 of the Mental Health Act 1983.

**4.**   Hoggett Mental Health Act op. cit. p.181-

**5.**   Dell S. Wanted an Insanity Defence that can be Used. [1983] Crim. L.R. 431 at page 434 and note 11.

**6.**   Law Commission Report (Law Comm. No. 177)(1989) paragraph 11.6 of Commentary in Vol II and Clause 35 of the Draft Criminal Code.

**7.**   *R. v. Hatt* [1962] Crim. L.R. 647.

**8.**   Butler Report op. cit. paragraph 18-35.

**9.**   [1973] 3 All E.R. 884.

130

**CHAPTER: 9 cont.**

10. [1973] 3 All E.R. 884 at 888.

12. *Unwin v. Hanson* [1891] 2 Q.B. 119 and *Bourne v. Norwich Crematorium Ltd.* [1967] 1 W.L.R. 691 at 695.

13. *W. v. L.* [1973] 3 All E.R. 884 at 890.

14. [1973] 3 All E.R. 884.

15. Butler Report op. cit. paragraph 18.35.

16. Griew E. "Let's Implement Butler on Mental Disorder and Crime" in Current Legal Problems 1984 p. 47 at p.56.

17. Butler Report op. cit. paragraph 18.35.

18. [1975] Q.B. 834, 841.

19. Kenny A. The Expert in Court (1983) 99 L.Q.R. 197.

20. [1960] 2 Q.B. 396, 404.

21. Butler Report op. cit. paragraph 18.18.

22. The Law Commission Report No. 177 (1989) Vol. I.

# INDEX

| | |
|---|---|
| Abnormality of mind | 16, 31 |
| Automatism | 19-21, 22 |
| Board of Control | 10 |
| Butler Committee | 13, 14, 16-19, 42, 45, 50 |
| Consent to treatment | 9, 52-57, 64 |
| Criminal Code | 47, 106, 112 |
| Crown Court | 11, 50, 58, 59, 69, 76, 77, 78 |
| Death penalty | 26, 39 |
| Detention | 9, 15, 25, 41, 50, 51, 79, 81, 91, 93, 94 |
| Diabetics | 20, 23, 24 |
| Diminished responsibility | 17, 26-33, 39-40 |
| Discharge | 12, 51 |
| Doctor | |
| - approved | 11, 13, 25, 51, 60 |
| - examination | 96 |
| - independent | 53, 61, 62, 63, 64 |
| - second opinion | 55-57 |
| Drunkenness | 21 |
| Durham Formula | 42 |
| Epilepsy | 22, 23 |
| European Convention on Human Rights | 50, 81, 94 |
| European Court of Human Rights | 44, 48, 50, 89, 91 |
| Fitness to plead | 24-25 |
| Gowers Commission | 6 |
| Guardianship | 58 |
| Home Secretary | 12, 13, 61, 66, 79, 80 |
| Homicide Act 1957 | 9, 10, 16, 17, 26, 29, 31, 37, 110 |
| Hospital managers | 58, 60, 63 |
| Hospital orders | 12, 25, 45, 58-75 |
| Insanity defence | 15-25, 36, 43, 45 |
| Interim hospital orders | 50 |
| Irresistible impulse | 34, 35, 111 |
| Jury | 2, 4, 5, 6, 7, 15, 17, 22, 25, 27-28, 30, 31, 39, 41, 42, 108 |
| Law Commission | 45, 47, 106, 112 |
| McNaghten Case | 3-6, 10, 16, 18, 23, 24, 25, 31, 34, 35, 42, 44, 45, 46, 47, 67, 104, 106, 110, 112 |
| Magistrates' Court | 59 |
| Manslaughter | 17, 26, 27, 28, 30, 37, 67 |
| Medical evidence | 6, 8, 27 |
| Medical recommendations | 60-63 |

Medical treatment                                              48, 52-57
Mental disorder                         10, 18, 25, 34, 38, 45, 46, 47
Mental Health Act (1983)   3, 10, 12, 14, 16, 18, 26, 32, 36, 44, 45,
   47, 51, 53, 54, 55, 58, 61, 64, 68, 69, 76, 77, 78, 79, 80, 82, 83,
   84, 87, 89, 90, 91, 92, 93, 94, 98, 99, 100, 101, 102, 103, 105, 107,
                                              108, 109, 110, 112
Mental Health Act Commission                           10, 55, 56
Mental Health Review Tribunals       10, 13, 49-51, 68, 80, 81
Mental illness                                                        58
Mental impairment                                                  58
MIND                                                             50, 82
Murder          2, 3, 9, 26, 28, 29, 30, 33, 36, 37, 39, 110
Nearest relative                                                     94
National Council for Civil Liberties                               14
Nurse                                                                56
Offences
   - basic intent                                                  20
   - specific intent                                        20, 36, 38
Old Bailey                                  1, 2, 83-87, 113, 115
Othello Syndrome                                                  27
Patient       9, 10, 12, 13, 32, 41, 44, 48, 49, 51-58, 61, 72, 76, 78,
                                           80-83, 87-103, 107-109
Percy Commission                                                  91
Prison transfer       3, 13, 14, 50, 50, 51-52, 61, 78, 82, 98, 103
Prosecution                              20, 27, 28, 31, 40, 106
Psychiatric probation order                                   18, 68
Psychopathic disorder                        10, 36, 42-44, 52
Radnor Commission                                               7, 8
Regional Hospital Authority powers                             65
Regional secure units                                             68
Release from hospital
   - by court                                               52, 69, 76
   - by Home Secretary                                 52, 67, 79, 81
   - by Mental Health Review Tribunal       14, 44, 79, 81, 82,
                                                       100, 102
Remand to hospital                                                50
Recklessness                                                  20, 21-24
Responsible Medical Officer                              55, 56, 78
Restriction direction                                             50
Restriction order                                      12, 66, 76-90
Royal College of Psychiatrists                             61, 109
Severe mental illness       16, 18, 42, 47, 104, 107, 108, 110, 112

133

Severe mental impairment 58
Severe subnormality 10, 48, 90, 104, 109
Sleep-walking 23
Special verdict 6, 23, 45, 90, 105, 110
Transfer direction 51-52
Treatment 8, 9, 12, 39, 40, 50, 52-57, 63, 71, 77, 102
World Health Organisation 16